Your People Will Be My People

Your People Will Be My People

A MEMOIR

by
SEBASTIAN BAKARE

foreword by Herman C. Waetjen

RESOURCE *Publications* · Eugene, Oregon

I dedicate this memoir to my loving parents Eric and Eunice Bakare and to my in-laws Hans and Magdalena Büchsel.

In gratitude for their love and care for our family.

Contents

Foreword

" **W**ho am I and where did I come from?" At some time in life, who does not ask these questions? Identity and origin are points of departure into life that begin with the uniqueness of ethnicity. However distant the circumstances of ethnic origin may be, the potentiality of identity and origin must eventually be tried and tested by confrontations with the realities of the world beyond the community of birth in order to be fulfilled. This is the story of Bishop Sebastian Bakare.

It begins with the uniqueness of his ethnicity. Born into the Bakare clan, he is distinguished by three totems: Dziwa, Sawe and Sambiri; and they combine to identify him and his ancestors as "the people from the river." His native history discloses migratory movements that originated in the Middle East, settling into the areas represented today by the present countries of Botswana, Transvaal, and Mozambique, and more eventually an exodus from Kwazulu Natal. Out of this ethnic inception Sebastian was born in Southern Rhodesia.

His grandparents were among the first generation of converts to Christianity in Makute, the mission village that was renamed Epiphany in Manicaland, a province of the colonial territory of the British Empire that initially was called "Southern Rhodesia." His maternal grandmother was baptized at the Epiphany Mission in 1891; his paternal grandmother, also among the first generation of converts, married a polygamist who became his grandfather. His parents, Eunice and Eric, accordingly, were second generation Christians. In that time missionaries gave them their Western names, and Sebastian's name was chosen by the Reverend Henry Glover, the Rector of the Epiphany Mission.

Sebastian was born in 1940, soon after World War II had begun, and his father was among the men who were conscripted by the colonial government to construct roads and bridges throughout the country without pay. He was the first-born in his family, but he was handed over to one of his grandmothers to give her his youthful company in her aging years. After she died, he rejoined his parents and his two younger brothers, but his life was different as he began to approach the end of the environmental circumstances of his ethnicity. He did not know that he would be forced out of Epiphany; he did not know that he would spend part of his childhood in Matabeleland; he did not know that he would become a priest and a bishop. As a black African, born into and suffering under the apartheid structures of Southern Rhodesia, he will be confronted with God's summons, "Whom shall I send?" And by responding again and again, "Here am I; send me!" he will be drawn into God's mission and ministry as a priest of the Anglican Church, accompanied by a German-born wife who, like the Moabite Ruth, will go where he goes, and will lodge where he lodges, and his people will be her people and his God will be her God, as they work together in national and international contexts for justice, equality and freedom.

An early experience of seeing a white man riding on a horse with an African on a bicycle behind him remained a disturbing memory for many years. It was not merely because he and his schoolmates saw a horse for the very first time. The man came to inform the elders of Epiphany that the village now belonged to a white farmer named Timmins, and Sebastian, his family and the entire community were given two weeks' notice to leave. No transport would be provided; they would have to go on foot and take with them whatever they could carry. They were reduced to refugees as they walked eighty kilometers to an unknown location. As he left his ethnic origin behind, he would continue to be haunted by the image of the white man seated on a horse.

In 1956, at the age of sixteen, the Reverend Ffrancon-Jones, who was the Rector of his boarding school, preached a sermon on Isaiah 6 in the context of Ghana, which had just attained its independence from British rule. He integrated God's calling of Isaiah into their contemporaneous African time and place, and challenged his students, "Your people are calling; they long to be liberated from oppressive British Rule." It ignited within Sebastian a commitment to God to devote his life to the liberation of his native land and its people. Inexplicably, as though it was being reinforced by God, Isaiah 6 would confront him with the same summons in all his ordination services as deacon, priest and bishop: "Whom shall I send? And who shall go for us?" And he would be challenged to make the same response at each installation: "Here am I. Send me!" Throughout his life Sebastian remained astonished at the reoccurrence of Isaiah 6 in three different venues.

Three years later when he was nineteen years old, Ffrancon-Jones asked him whether he had ever thought about the priesthood. Even before he replied, the Rector took the initiative and applied for Sebastian to be admitted to St. John's Seminary in Lusaka, Northern Rhodesia. There he began his studies in January 1960. His experience of this grace on his behalf became a distinguishing originality in his life. Sebastian never contended for himself; he never publicized or magnified himself. God was beginning to open doors for him, one after another, and he gratefully walked through them in order to serve God and fulfill his divine call. He was ordained as a deacon at the age of twenty-one on December 8, 1961 and two years later as a priest on December 17, 1963, and he began to actualize his ministry as a curate to the Msoro Mission of Northern Rhodesia and subsequently to St. Cyprians in the Copper-belt region of the country. After some extraordinary years in his early priesthood, he left Northern Rhodesia as it gained its independence of Great Britain and became Zambia, and he entered into a graduate program of study in education at the University of Birmingham in England.

In 1968 Sebastian attended the Assembly of the World Council of Churches in Uppsala, Sweden where he met Christians from all over the world. For the first time in his young life he was introduced to the world-wide horizon of the gospel's inclusivity, and, with students from five continents, he served as a steward. Among them was a young woman from Gelsenkirchen, Germany, Ruth Büchsel. He called her Rut, and she impressed him by her integrity, her generosity, and her knowledge of the larger issues of the world. They became friends and began to exchange letters after his return to Birmingham. Later in that year she invited him to come to Germany for Christmas, and, as reluctant as he was to go because he did not speak German, he accepted anyway. He was welcomed by her father, Hans Büchsel, a Lutheran pastor in Gelsenkirchen, and her mother, Magdalena, and he was grateful to spend more time with Rut. When she visited him later in Birmingham, they realized that they were committed to each other. He stopped in Gelsenkirchen on his way back to Zambia, proposed marriage to her, and they celebrated their engagement with her family and friends. Getting married in Germany, however, posed a problem when Rhodesia refused to give him a birth certificate, and he and Rut were constrained to choose a civil marriage in Zambia and a church wedding in Germany.

Rut joined him after he returned to Zambia, and, by her selflessness, courage, trust, and specifically by her commitment to work with him in the fulfillment of his priesthood, she showed herself to be a personification of the biblical figure of Ruth. But they could not enter his homeland because Rhodesia had terminated his passport. Constrained to return to Germany, he became an instructor in comparative religion in Versmold, teaching himself German, until he was invited to become a co-pastor in a German Lutheran church. The national media were captivated by an African priest engaged in the pastoral care of a German congregation and featured him and his ministry in a TV film that was broadcast throughout the country. During this time in Germany their first daughter, Nyasha was born, and three years later their daughter Tinao.

Within those five years he traveled with a study group to the United States to learn what denominational seminaries were doing to promote continuing education, and these diversified experiences expanded his international acclimatization. At the Graduate Theological Union in Berkeley, he enjoyed a congenial relationship with the faculty of the Church Divinity School of the Pacific, and it emerged into an invitation to return to undertake a Master's degree in theology and it included the grace of financial support that would enable his family to accompany him.

Zimbabwe became independent in 1980, and Sebastian, now forty years old, flew to Salisbury (soon to be renamed Harare) to cast his vote. He had left Rhodesia in the innocence of his youth, and now he was returning in the maturity of an internationally acclimatized priest who had married the daughter of a German Lutheran pastor, engaged in a ministry in Germany, and together with his wife had gained advanced degrees from two of the finest academic institutions in the world.

But he was coming home to Zimbabwe without a job. During his exile in Germany, he had been an active supporter of ZANU, the liberation movement that began to govern Zimbabwe at its independence. He was offered the deputy directorship of the office of National Cooperatives, but the objective of his return was to actualize his priesthood in Zimbabwe in order to fulfill the mandate that had been given to him through the reading of Isaiah 6 at his ordinations as deacon and priest. He was compelled to accept a part-time chaplaincy for the Anglican students at the university, an appointment as co-rector of All Souls in Mount Pleasant, and a part-time lectureship in the university's Religious Studies Department. Their third daughter Rufaro was born in the Mbuya Nehanda Maternity Ward during that time, and Rut's parents, Opa and Oma, flew from Germany to be present at her baptism.

Sebastian became the Urban and Rural Mission Secretary in the Zimbabwe Council of Churches in 1984, and it familiarized him with every corner of the country where a church was located. Notably it evoked in him a joyful sense of serving God's people in an ecumenical setting in his homeland, and Isaiah 6 continued to inspire him with its summons, "Your people are calling!" The position he had been hoping for materialized in 1984, and he was chosen to be the ecumenical chaplain of the University of Zimbabwe. It proved to be a demanding office as there were continued crises between the university students and the Zimbabwean government. Many of the students came from poor families in rural areas of Zimbabwe and they were raising their voices about critical issues about the country's political and economic policies. Their protests and demonstrations evoked bitterness and hostility between them and the police. As chaplain, Sebastian had to place himself between these antagonistic groups in efforts to achieve justice and conciliation.

In 1980 the Anglican Church of Zimbabwe formed the Diocese of Manicaland, and Sebastian was elected its second bishop in 1999. To be the chief shepherd of God's flock appeared to be an overwhelming responsibility, and initially he said no. But his self-understanding as a priest had been formed by his identification with Isaiah's response to God's call and, like Isaiah, he accepted, "Here am I. Send me." Now, as bishop, he could work more forcefully to liberate his people from their subjugation to poverty, hunger, disease, corruption, inequality, selfishness, oppression, and human rights. This involvement was reinforced by his ongoing international travels. As a member of the Anglican Standing Commission on Mission and Evangelism, he was required to visit many of its twenty-two Anglican provinces to promote dynamic Mission and Evangelism programs in justice, critical health issues, and the elimination of poverty.

During this time his wife Rut became deeply involved in advancing the work of the Mothers Union, a guild of the Anglican Church that had about 3,000 members in the diocese. In her capacity as a theologian and educator she organized leadership training sessions in every district and commissioned those who participated to go and teach others about the important role of mothers in their families and communities. When the training sessions were completed in all the districts, she called for a Mothers Union convention in August 2000, and more than 3,000 women attended the convention that was held at St. Augustine's Mission in Penhalonga.

After his retirement as bishop, he accepted a lectureship at Africa University to teach Systematic Theology and Professional Ethics, but it was short-lived. He was called to be the caretaker bishop of the Diocese of Harare to replace its bishop, Nolbert Kunonga, who was degrading his office and prostituting his congregation by his collaboration with Robert Mugabe, the corrupt president of Zimbabwe. Sebastian, with the support of the majority of the members of the Diocese, organized meetings in house churches, both in the city and its residential areas; and he filed a lawsuit with the High Court to have the church buildings returned to the Diocese. Kunonga rejected the court's ruling, and promoted the harassment and arrests of those who were following Sebastian as their caretaker bishop, while the police continued to force themselves into their churches during the Sunday services of worship.

Rut, however, working with the Mothers Union, organized women to meet in houses and other places where Kunonga had no access. After supervising leadership training sessions for selected individuals, she formed an all-day meeting for the Mothers Union to meet in the safety of St. Michael's church in Mbare, and about 800 women attended. As she was finishing her presentation, however, four trucks loaded with riot police drove up and tear-gassed the meeting, ending it abruptly. Unknown to them, a crew from German television was present, secretly filming the proceedings, and already that very evening the aggression of the Harare police was being televised in Germany. Christians, persecuted in their own church, were being publicized internationally.

Sebastian and Rut's collaborative ministry throughout their married years reached a momentous and unexpected climax in 2008 when Sebastian was awarded the Swedish Par Anger prize in Sweden. Established in 2004 to promote the struggle for justice, human rights, and democracy, it is awarded by the Swedish government to honor Ambassador Per Anger who had risked his life to assist Jews to leave Germany secretly during World War II. It was given to him in Stockholm, the city in which he and Rut had met each other in 1968. Sebastian was honored with an evening of speeches, and he had an opportunity to share stories of the atrocities that were being committed by the Mugabe government.

During the two years that followed, Sebastian and Rut were honored for their service to the church in Zimbabwe and the wider world by being awarded honorary doctorates from two Episcopalian seminaries. The first was given in 2009 by the Church Divinity School of the Pacific in Berkeley, the seminary that had awarded them two years of graduate study in 1982-1984, and the other a year later by the General Theological Seminary in New York. Sebastian had the blessed joy of baptizing their granddaughter, Nomsa Elizabeth, the child of their oldest daughter Nyasha and her husband Alain, at St. Mark's Episcopal Church in Brooklyn.

Sebastian ends his Memoir with an address to "My dear 'Born Frees', and by that, I mean my Zimbabwe brothers and sisters who were born knowing only independence." He reviews for them the history of his experience from Rhodesia into Zimbabwe and confronts them with the illusion of Zimbabwe as a free and liberated country. In the face of all the suffering and pain that he endured, he concludes with a personal word of his own grief and hope.

> "I stand at a crossroads between life and death but for now, the window remains open and I can still see the endless horizon. I am convinced that God will take me to my destination when that moment comes. Meanwhile, I look forward each day to new experiences as they come within my reach. So far, my journey has provided me with joyful moments and sad – the saddest being the untimely passing on of "my dear companion, Rut. I miss her every day."

Ruth Büchsel, his beloved wife and companion Rut for 48 years, died on October 21, 2017. Together Sebastian and Rut fulfilled God's call throughout their united response to Isaiah 6, "Here I am. Send me!" Their integrated life in mission and ministry glorified God and God honored them.

Herman C. Waetjen
Robert S. Dollar Professor Emeritus of New Testament
San Francisco Theological Seminary
Graduate Theological Union

Preface

" Don't urge me to leave you or to turn from you. Where you go, I will go, and where you stay I will stay. Your people will be my people and your God my God. Where you die, I will die, and there I will be buried. Your God will be my God and your people my people. (*Ruth 1*).

In the Old Testament, Ruth has a deep devotion to her mother-in-law and God. She is a Moabite—a gentile—while her mother-in-law is a Jew. Ruth's going to a foreign land—foreign in every way, including culture, race, language, and religion, is a call for her to undertake. She trusts in God. As she says, Your God will be my God.

Rut (in German, or Reuthe in Hebrew) means companion partner, friend; the Biblical Ruth was all this to her mother-in-law Naomi who she followed, after the death of her husband, when Naomi wanted to go across the Moabite bridge back to her native land of Judah.

Like the Ruth in the Bible, Rut, my companion, friend, and partner, was ready to cross several bridges:

Between the southern and northern hemispheres;

Between Africa and Europe—the continents and the races;

Between the Shona and German languages;

Between Anglicanism and Lutheranism.

Together, the two of us were to crisscross the global village where people of different races and cultures are still set against one another.

Crossing any bridge demands trust and confidence in the constructors of the bridge. Our faith in God whose incarnate Son constructed an everlasting, reconciling bridge between God and humanity inspires us. On our journey, we were privileged to encounter pilgrims engaged in a similar task to unite people in Christ. "Behold I make all things new" (Revelation 21:5)," "where there is neither Jew nor gentile, neither slave nor free, neither male nor female" (Galatians 3:28). In our context, there is no black or white, for all are one in Christ Jesus. Rut and I were in solidarity with fellow Christians who were no longer captives of their culture or skin color, but liberated and engaged in disbanding systems that divide people. "Your people will be my people and your God my God. Where you die I will die, and there will be buried." Rut lived the promise of the biblical Ruth to the end by becoming a mother to many Zimbabweans and is now resting in peace in the Great Anglican Cathedral of St. Mary's and All Saints in Harare, the capital city. "Where you die, I will die and there will be buried."

To you my daughters: Nyasha, Tinao, and Rufaro, and Nomsa, my grandchild, and the yet unborn, and whoever reads this memoir, I commend the memory of your mother, grandmother, and friend in hopes that you will find ways in your life contexts to emulate her example by holding on to Christ the Great Bridge that reconciles and binds with God.

Acknowledgments

My memoir would be incomplete without expressing my heartfelt gratitude to a crowd of witnesses who have physically and spiritually been with me and Ruth on our pilgrimage. Your partnership, support, and friendship, or your just being there have been consistent and indispensable.

To Dr. Linda Chipunza, Mainini, you remained Rut's prayerful partner to the end. Your sermon at her memorial service in the Cathedral of St. Mary's and All Saints said it all. You are truly Mainini to my daughters and me and we shall always call you Mainini because of your genuine love.

To Professor John Pobee, my dear brother, you crossed the international bridge from Ghana to find Rut your sister in Zimbabwe. She truly became your sister just as I became a brother to your wife, Her Excellency Martha Pobee. What a solid bridge we built between us! Both you and Rut have crossed the last bridge and are now resting eternally in God's Glory, yet we remain spiritually connected. John, I hear your voice through the several books you authored that you gave me. What a legacy I inherited from you.

To Professor Herman and Mary Waetjen: Your profound friendship, love, and the words in your message of condolence on Rut's passing touched us immensely. Herman, your intellectual and insightful theological advice became a strong pillar for me to lean on when I wrote my doctoral dissertation "My Right to Land." You led me and brought me to a different horizon in my theological outlook and I benefited immensely from your scholarship. I remain grateful to you and Mary for your generosity and hospitality during my doctoral studies at San Francisco Theological Seminary.

To Harriet Linville, my contemporary at Church Divinity School of the Pacific, for deploying your English Literature expertise by going through my memoir. Thank you, Harriet. What a great friend you have been to me and Rut since our time together in Berkeley to the present.

ACKNOWLEDGMENTS

To Professors Chris and Jane Mutambirwa: You played an admirable role in our pilgrimage. Although Rut is no longer among us, I sincerely appreciate your unwavering love, care, and friendship. You are Auntie Jane and Uncle Chris to my daughters and I cherish the relationship that exists. You remain Maiguru and Babamunini for me as long as we walk together on our earthy journey. I enjoy and love your company and fellowship

To Dorothy and Jimmy Khatso, thank you for your profound and boundless love, care, and friendship. My daughters call you Auntie Dorothy and Uncle Jimmy and that is, indeed, who you are to them. They know how close you were to their mother. You are in touch with them to this day, and I am so grateful to you for your weekly calls to touch base. Being on my own, such calls make me feel much loved and cared for. Your home has become my second home in Harare and your hospitality is so dear to me.

To Shelagh Millar, my dear friend, your love for Rut was exceptional. You came all the way from Forfar, Scotland to bid farewell to your dear Rut at her funeral. On that day, your presence in the Cathedral of St. Mary's and All Saints was a great testimony of how much Rut meant to you. Then, you came a second time for Rut's memorial service and delivered a touching eulogy. You are an exceptional friend to the family; not many friends can do what you did. Yours was a demonstration of genuine friendship, a blessing, and a source of encouragement to the children and me. I now continue on my journey without Rut but in the company of trustworthy partners like you.

To Hans-Herman and Dorothee, my dear brother-in-law and sister-in-law, your steadfast love and care for my family are boundless. Hans-Herman, and your sister Elizabeth, have been staunch pillars for us since 1968. For forty-eight years we walked so happily together and enjoyed each other's company and we continue to do so even now without Rut. You are exceptional in-laws.

To His Excellency the Ambassador of Australia, Matthew Neuhaus, and his wife Angela: Rut and I were excited when you accepted our invitation to come and officially open our clinic at Nedziwe. Your donation of a ward for expectant mothers was highly appreciated and your name on the plaque bears testimony of your mission of goodwill to Zimbabwe.

To Andrew Kadel, my contemporary at The Divinity School of the Pacific: You welcomed me to your parish in the Bronx and I felt very much at home. You and Paula hosted me for a week in your lovely flat where I enjoyed beautiful views of the Hudson River and New York City.

ACKNOWLEDGMENTS

To Paula Schaap: This memoir would have been unthinkable without your editing expertise. What a mammoth task you accepted to undertake. You devoted a lot of your time to it. In editing my memoir, you made my story and Rut more meaningful to me, my daughters, Nomsa, and friends who will read it.

To The Rt. Rev'd. Christopher Bishop of Southwark: My memoir would be incomplete without me mentioning your care for Rut. When she lost a pair of her hearing aid, you did not hesitate to take her to an audiologist where you paid a lot of money for an expensive new pair she used for many years until she passed on, we had taken this trip to London without medical cover, faced with this situation, you readily played the role of a good friend but above all the role of a good Shepherd befitting your call. Rut and I were touched by your sense of care, love, and generosity.

To my daughters, Nyasha, Tinao, and Rufaro, thank you, thank you, for being such caring daughters. This memoir came into being because of your pushing me to write a story about me and your mother. It has not been so easy; the passing on of your mother has and still is very fresh in my mind. I did try to write down what I thought could be useful to you, but above all as a small legacy to my grandchildren.

To Nyasha and Alain: You hosted me for a year and three months in your lovely home in Hopewell, New Jersey, where I enjoyed the environment and quiet atmosphere to write without distraction. Your home provides a wonderful atmosphere that is conducive to writing; it's not surprising that my granddaughter Nomsa started writing books at a very early stage. The environment of your home helped me recall some of the people and landmarks; memories I needed to complete my memoir.

To Tinao and Julius: Your home has a grandeur that offers a most welcome atmosphere, and every time I visit I feel very much at home. Sitting on your spacious veranda, looking at your garden and the trees around, give me an appreciative sense of the beauty of Zimbabwe. Thank you for hosting me all the time I come to your home.

To Ruffi: Thank you for your ideas and suggestions at the very beginning of my memoir. Also, for making use of your privilege as a Lufthansa staff member to facilitate several trips for your mother and me to travel to and from Zimbabwe to the United States and Europe. We were able to see several European countries and some places in the U.S. which wouldn't have been possible without your assistance. Once, when we were stranded on our way to Frankfurt a kind colleague helped us, and then we had a lovely hotel you had booked for us to help us forget about our travel woes.

To Nomsa: When I was trying to figure out an introduction for my memoir, I came to a point when I just couldn't think any further. I came down from my room and found you in the middle of writing your book; you inspired me. I said to myself if Nomsa can write not only a book, but many books, why couldn't I? You inspired and motivated me. The title of my memoir is about your Oma saying what "your people will be my people." Thank you, Nomie, for having inspired me. God bless and inspire your writing as you grow up.

CHAPTER ONE

Beginnings and a Call

In the beginning, I am faced with the question of identity. Put simply: "Who am I and where did I come from?"

In Zimbabwe, we identify each other by the totem of one's clan. When a woman marries, she retains her totem with her.

I belong to the Bakare clan, which has three totems, or spirit symbols: The Dziwa, Sawe, and Sambiri.

Daiwa means a pool—very often referring to living water—where amphibians such as frogs, crocodiles, or hippopotamuses can afford to live a double life, while fish confine themselves to Dziwa, their permanent habitation. Dziwa is the kingdom of the crocodiles; if human beings stray into their domain, crocodiles would make a feast out of them. The River Rusingapwi, which means the perennial river, that ran through my birthplace, Epiphany, was free from crocodiles and so we children could enjoy our *samba* (swim) without fear. We grew up being true children of the river.

Sawe is the name of a river that flows between Manicaland and Mashonaland, East Provinces, into the Indian Ocean. According to a traditional story, when our forebears escaped from KwaZulu Natal, they went northeast and ended up in Mozambique, where they followed a river called Sawe. They hid as they went along the river, most likely spending some time walking along the banks like amphibian creatures, emerging on land where they felt safer because the river was, and still is, infested with vicious crocodiles. (Many Zimbabweans crossing the Limpopo River to South Africa have been victims of those crocodiles.) My forebears were nicknamed "the people from the river," meaning the river Sawe and that became the totem of the clan.

The word Sambiri comes from two words: *samba,* meaning to wash, and *mbiri,* meaning famous swimming people.

Some people might construe these stories as myth, but as in every myth, there is always a grain of truth. I am convinced that a long distance on foot from KwaZulu Natal to Zimbabwe via Mozambique, more than 2,000 kilometers, had many dangers involved, whether you went along the banks of the river or inland.

Dziwa, Sawe, and Sambiri: all my identities are related to water. My totems are used as pleasantries when people greet each other; when people meet or before they sit down to discuss business. At the end of their business, they bid farewell to the host, saying, "Goodbye, Sawe (or Dziwa or Sambiri)," or "Thank you, Dziwa," as a sign of appreciation by mentioning the totem. This is how the practice was kept alive and handed down to my generation. To be addressed by one's totem is a sign of respect.

Traditionally, I belong to a migrant clan who, according to oral tradition, came from the Middle East in the 18th century through Munomutapa's kingdom which, at that time, covered Botswana, Transvaal, and Mozambique where the majority of my forebears settled. But three Bakare brothers continued to KwaZulu Natal. Probably the Dziwa clan had some conflict or feud which caused the brothers to leave their home and go somewhere far away to start a new life. This was a common occurrence among tribes at that time. Whenever there was a misunderstanding, some of the family would move away from the village, local area, district, or province, and that was considered the best solution to keep the peace. Sometimes, when a family member decided to move away from the clan because of fights, they would even change the surname but not the totem.

In 1986, when I was chaplain at the University of Zimbabwe, Dr. S.M. Mutsvairo, a faculty member, invited me to his office. He was very keen to know whether the Bakares, who he knew with a totem of Dziwa, were my relatives. I confirmed that it was my clan. In a follow-up conversation at his home, he talked to me about my ancestors' exodus from KwaZulu Natal. He was the one who explained to me that there were some tribal/clan rivalries in KwaZulu Natal around 1823, before the Berlin Conference, where the European powers divided up Africa, which resulted in many families leaving the province. Some ended up in Matabeleland and Gazaland (today

Chipinge), after traveling via Mozambique. Dr. S.M. Mutsvairo said that in KwaZulu my totem is Ngwenya, which means crocodile.

He went on to tell me that a small group of my forebears came via Gazaland. Although they were three brothers and good fighters, they were also afraid to get into conflict with the local populations, so they trekked along the banks of the river Sawe. One brother settled in Chimoio in Mozambique near Beira; the second in Mutasa near Mutare; and the third in Makoni district, Rusape (Manicaland). The third is my direct ancestor. My forebears, being good fighters, were awarded by the local chiefs with wives and leadership positions at the head of their *limbs*, which were small army groups. Dr. S.M. Mutsvairo said that, unfortunately, in these societies with an oral tradition, nothing was written down for the benefit of future generations. I hope that in the future, one member of the Dziwa/Sawe/Sambiri clan will be inspired to do some research on the origin and migration of the clan from the Middle East to Zimbabwe.

Dr. S.M. Mutswairo is famous as the author of the poem that was chosen as Zimbabwe's national anthem. At the end of our discussion about my clans, I asked him the meaning of his poem; he said that it was his prayer for Zimbabwe, the land of our forebears.

Dr. S. M. Mutswairo is now resting in God's Glory. He is greatly missed but will be remembered by our generation and generations to come whenever they sing the national anthem:

> O lift the banner,
> the flag of Zimbabwe,
> the symbol of freedom proclaiming victory
> The land of our fathers bestowed upon us all.

* * *

To my surprise, Isaiah Chapter 6 was read at all my ordination services: deacon, priest, and bishop. It has been a constant throughout my life of service to God's people, and especially, to my native land, Zimbabwe.

In this passage, Isaiah sits in the Temple, and hears the voice of the Lord saying, "Who shall I send? And who shall go for us?" And Isaiah said, "Here am I. Send me!"

When I was sixteen, I heard this text preached by the Rector and Principal of my boarding school, the Reverend Ffrancon-Jones, on the Sunday of the week that Ghana attained self-rule from Britain—March 6, 1957—and the people of Ghana were celebrating their independence.

Toward the end of his sermon, Reverend Ffrancon-Jones brought the prophecy of Isaiah up to the present time and place. He said to us students, "Your people are calling; they long to be liberated from the oppressive British Rule."

Reverend Ffrancon-Jones was a Welsh theologian and a nationalist at heart who resented British rule in his country of Wales. (I only learned later as a student in Birmingham, England, that Wales had been fighting to gain autonomy from the United Kingdom for years when a group of Welsh nationalists blew up a water pipeline in a part of that city.)

Those words from our Rector and Principal on that day in 1956, "Your people are calling," remained in my mind all my life. It led me to my vocation to the ordained ministry. How this Bible chapter was repeatedly chosen at my ordination remains a mystery to me to this day, because my ordination services to the diaconate and priesthood took place at different places, years, and times in Zambia. Then, years later, when I was ordained bishop in Zimbabwe, it was read again.

At each of these services, the ordinand is asked by the bishop to answer questions as laid out in the ordination liturgy, including, "Do you believe, so far as you know your own heart, that God has called you to the office and work of a deacon /priest/bishop in his Church?" The response is, "I believe that God has called me." I agreed to be ordained to go and serve God's people at each of these three ordination services. But little did I understand about the cost of discipleship. I thought that my call was to preach the gospel in a peaceful situation.

Isaiah was called at a time when neighboring nations were on the march to annihilate Judah. The Northern Kingdom of Israel with its headquarters in Samaria had been captured by the Assyrian army and the captives dispersed all over Syrian provinces in the North. The Northern Kingdom of Israel with its headquarters in Samaria was no more; Judah in the South, with its capital in Jerusalem was the next to be annexed. Now with the imminent invasion coming, Isaiah's response "Here am I, send me," was an acceptance of a steep call. He sounded naïve, but he was not. He was only too aware that Judah's army was not a match for Nebuchadnezzar's army. The only option left for him was to warn the leadership of Judah about God's pending judgment because of their idolatrous behavior.

Isaiah's deep sense of vocation impressed me and had a direct impact on my life. The words "your people are calling you" never left me and they continued to resonate strongly in my mind through my training in the priesthood at St. John's Seminary. Sometimes, I thought that I was becoming crazy or insane because I could not let go of the words "Your people are calling you."

Unlike Isaiah, I became a deacon and then was ordained to the priesthood when the Federation of Rhodesia and Nyasaland was showing some signs of instability, although not to the same level of devastation as when Nebuchadnezzar invaded Judah. I thought my ministry was going to be in a relatively calm region. I felt that my mission to serve God's people would be to preach the gospel of peace and justice to the oppressor and the oppressed. A call to serve my people was very welcome, although it had its challenges. Law enforcement agents could be vicious, and arrests were made at random for flimsy reasons.

* * *

In 1939 my parents were married, first in an African traditional marriage where the groom paid the bride's family a *lobola*, or what might be called a "bride price," which could be several farm animals. This tradition was used to express the joining of two families. Later, they had a church blessing. This was surely the wrong time for my parents to be married as that was the year World War II broke out and would soon engulf the entire world. Yet they married!

My mother's maiden name was Eunice Nyakadumba. The Nyakadumba family lived in a village called Nyamutowa some ten kilometers from Epiphany, my father's home, which was also the center of the district's mission church. My paternal grandmother's Christian name was Lilian; she was among the first generation of converts in the country. Although she was already a Christian, she married my grandfather, who was a polygamist with several wives. My father was the only child of my grandmother with her polygamous husband; my paternal grandfather did not live long enough to see me.

At that time, parents did not choose names for their children at baptism, so my father, being the only son of his mother, was named Eric, meaning the only one. As for my grandfather, because he died before I was born, all I could see was a cave in a nearby mountain where he was buried that was a traditional cemetery for the Bakare clan. According to traditional beliefs, burial places, whether in the ground or in a cave, were revered and considered sacred. Children were told not to go near the mouth of such a cave so as not to disturb the sleepers within. As children, we were told that if we came too close and looked into the cave, we risked losing our sight and then would never find our way back home. Or we might even become insane! Since, of course, we did not want to go blind, or become insane, we never dared to come close to the cave in order to see what was inside.

Once on a summer day in Somerset, England, I was shocked to see some youngsters heaping their jackets on tombstones as they were playing their games. I thought of my upbringing in Zimbabwe where such a thing could never happen; until this day, I don't feel comfortable touching a tombstone except for those of my family members. It's amazing how one's upbringing influences one's later life.

More than ten years after Zimbabwe's independence, when the government of Robert Mugabe was seizing white-owned farms, the minister in charge of that program, who happened to be a distant relative, asked me if I wanted a farm. My response was a big "No!" But he told me, whether I liked it or not, he was going to give me a piece of land below and around the mountain where my grandfather and other Bakare forebears were buried as part of my birthright. (I had published a book with the title "My Right to Land," about the how the land was stolen from the African peoples by white settlers, and he used the title of my book to say I could not turn down my birthright.) As I wasn't a farmer, I passed on this thirty-hectare piece of land near the Bakare clan cemetery to my nephew and he is still farming it. He has now been reconnected to the ancestral spiritual bond which had been broken between the living and the living dead during the settlers' invasion seventy years ago.

According to African tradition, the cemetery and those buried in the cave or ground were considered untouchable and sacred, so when Africans were evicted from their traditional land, leaving behind their sacred burial places, spirituality between the living and the living dead was broken. The African traditional religion conception of the living dead is taken very seriously, even by Christians. It reminds me of the children of Israel, escaping from slavery in Egypt, who carried Joseph's bones with them to be buried in Shechem in the Promised Land (Joshua 24:32). Unlike the children of Israel, leaving behind their living dead was painful and unforgivable.

The Old Church in Epiphany (once named Makute) has remained with its original structure and mural paintings since 1891. Though its doors were closed for seventy years, there is now a resident priest, serving return-ees to the area. The British settler had been told to leave the farm he took by force from the indigenous peoples seventy years ago.

* * *

The word *mukute* is the name of a tree that produces a fruit called *hute*. The fruit has a shape like a plum and is very sweet. It ripens during the rainy season. The tree is found in the wetlands or semi-dry wetlands found in many parts of Manicaland. Our village was called Makute because it was littered with these trees. The hute can be harvested in large quantities for storage, but only for a short period before it becomes too soft and begins to ferment. There are other fruit trees like walnut and fig trees in the area, but mukute was dominant and popular.

Land in Epiphany was fertile and gave us the bulk of our staple food such as maize, *rapoko*, (finger millet), sorghum, rice, sweet potatoes, pump-kins, watermelons, *tsenza* (a root crop like sweet potatoes), wild mush-rooms. Besides that, there were nutritious termites and caterpillars, and plenty of fish from the Rusingapwi River, so-named because it never ran dry and brought water to the entire region.

As children we enjoyed swimming in the river naked; we did not have swimming costumes in those days like today. I feel very nostalgic when I think about it now—that I learned to swim in a pool with running water, where one could watch every movement of the fish. An exciting pastime, indeed! You could watch fish for as long as you were able to hold your breath underwater; then pop up to get fresh air; and this went on and on until one had enough. I often went home with red eyes after swimming underwater with wide-open eyes, so I could watch the river's occupants. One could see them very close, different sizes of tiny fishes in *mudungwe* (queues) running away, (hence the name madungwe, meaning small fish.) They moved in several queues, facing one direction towards the deeper and darker end of the pool. This pool—our pool—had a natural formation of a rocky wall with some stones protruding outward, creating a niche where small fish could swim in circles. Such a beautiful sight.

On one particular day, I became so fascinated watching a slightly big-ger fish follow a shoal of small fish heading to the darker corner of the pool, that I bashed the right side of my face against a stone. I came out crying, blood gushing down on my face. My cousin Naison, being all of twelve-years-old, felt responsible that he had let me swim towards the dark side of the pool. He staunched the bloody bruise with a leaf pulled from a nearby bush, and then applied liquid from a cactus leaf that acted as a natural band-aid. By the time I got home, the blood had stopped, and I tried to hide the bruised side of my face from my grandmother, fearing that, should she see it, I would not be allowed to go and swim again for some time. Luckily, she never saw that side of my face that was above my ear, partly hidden by my hair.

When Naison was about nineteen, he was working in his first job as a messenger for an insurance company in Bulawayo, the second-largest city in Zimbabwe, (still Rhodesia at the time), when he was killed by a gang of thieves. The police did not bother to investigate the crime; after all, he was an African, killed in an African neighborhood.

The river was about half a kilometer away from the village. Upstream was a small reservoir, protected from animals, which was used as a well for drinking water. There were enough open places along the river with easy access for animals to drink from. A rocky place with flat stones on the edge of the river was used by women for washing clothes, with enough space to dry the clothes on part of the rock, as well as spreading them on small bushes. There were two swimming pools downstream; one for girls and the other for boys.

When I was born cameras did not exist in our part of the world. How I have often wished to have in my possession some family photos—of myself as a toddler and as a small boy swimming in the river—or in my early teens. The only photo in my possession from my childhood was taken at a boarding school when I was a teenager.

Baptism in those days was a big Christian event. Children were baptized on Epiphany Day, the sixth of January, which was the day I was christened.

Sunday by Sunday, the converted and those preparing to be christened met in fellowship with each other the whole day. On Sunday, there were no social activities for children–apart from playing around the church. Our church when I was a child was under the leadership of Henry Glover, a white missionary who was very much loved by all the village. By sheer coincidence, when I chaired a Commission and Evangelism meeting in Johannesburg in 2003, I met Henry Glover's son who had since become a bishop in South Africa. We talked about his late father and what a lovable priest he was.

Zimbabwe, which means the House of Stone after the palace that housed the region's kings, is a country that has experienced a series of land invasions from the Portuguese, African warlords, the British, and then the white settler farmers. Long before I was born the British had already taken occupation of the country by force and I was, therefore, born under the established colonial system.

But when I was born, on November 1, 1940, the whole world was in the grips of an invasion called World War II. I try to imagine how my mother, a young woman, felt as she expected me, her first child, during a worldwide war. Surely, her anxiety must have been boundless. The war in Europe affected Africans as the men were recruited from the colonies to fight a war that was not their own. After the war ended, there was a different kind of invasion. At the end of the war, my parents told me how frightened they were when small places like Rusape and Nyazura, in Manicaland Province, were suddenly overwhelmed by white people of different European nationalities: Poles, Greeks, Italians, and English–both refugees and war veterans. They were now arriving in the country in frightfully large numbers, ready to settle in Rhodesia, now a British property. Southern Africa was known to have a favorable climate where white settlers could start a new life. But that meant that the native people were forced off their land that had been in their families for generations. Evictions after the war continued in earnest, with Africans being forcibly settled in arid regions that were not ideal for farming.

All this I didn't know as a baby, because all that was important to me was my mother's milk. What I didn't realize was that the men around me were experiencing increasingly harsh and merciless treatment. My father and many of his kinsmen and neighbors were conscripted for *corvée* (forced labor) to construct roads and bridges throughout the country against their will and without pay. They were not even fed for their labor.

When life begins to unfold itself at birth, it is like a window that opens and allows you to see the expanse of the horizon as far as your sight can allow. This window opens bit by bit and one sees more. What I see through the window is an endless space with a horizon at the end that is a fathomless void. The window can reveal what my natural eyes can view but what is beyond remains nothing, as long as I cannot see. And it is like a joy that one feels when watching the sunset as it disappears behind the horizon; although it will be dark in Zimbabwe, we know that it continues to shine in other parts of the world.

CHAPTER TWO

Eviction from Epiphany

It was two years after World War II officially ended with the surrender of Japan. One day in the afternoon when we children were playing soccer, we saw an unfamiliar sight. A white man was riding on a brown animal toward our village with an African man on a bicycle behind him. We had never seen a horse before—what a sight! The appearance of a horse and a white man created a sensation among us children; we were so very curious about it. We immediately abandoned our game and rushed home to get closer to this strange sight. We giggled as we stood at a distance from the white man, who, because of his trousers, appeared to us to be without knees. And that brown animal—the horse—was so much taller than our bulls in our pens.

The only white person we knew, before this strange appearance, was Father Henry Glover, but he rode a bicycle, not a horse. And he was a kind man—sometimes he played soccer with us, but as he could not run fast, his team always lost.

But this man was different from our priest; he had no manners. To this day, I remember him seated on his horse—the African officer beside him to interpret—speaking to the elders who were seated on the ground, as though they were children. This settler's attitude was that our elders were like children, and he did not need to show them respect.

The message he bought was that Epiphany now belonged to a white farmer by the name of Timmins and that he had come to give them two weeks' notice to leave. The place for the villagers' new settlement would be given by a district messenger from the native commissioner in Rusape.

Meanwhile, this man said, you have to prepare what to take with you. There is no transport—you will go on foot. It sounded like a punishment in the ears of us children and our elders. It was a command given to a people who had lost not only their land and their country, but their rights as well. The villagers were not given a chance to ask questions. The cortège left for Rusape; mission accomplished.

I remember vividly that we were left sitting as we always did in church: men on the right side and women on the left. But now, we were all quiet, stunned, confused. Our elders had no legal recourse to turn to for appeal because the traditional authorities of headmen and the chiefs had been stripped away. The Commissioner in Rusape, who had sent the white man and the African interpreter with the bad news, had the ultimate authority.

1947 shall forever be remembered by many Zimbabweans as a year of forced relocation, especially in Manicaland Province. World War II was over and there was a lot of movement of peoples, especially from Britain to the colonies. Rhodesia was considered an ideal and prime colony for white adventurous artisans and war veterans to settle. They came into the country in great numbers causing more relocation for the natives from their traditional and ancestral settlements. The most affected areas were those with fertile soil and favorable climate.

Makoni District up to the Nyanga region was declared New England. I was seven years old when that latest invasion took place. It was a dehumanizing experience for my parents and us children. Even as a young child, I became conscious of what an unjust system it was, especially as there was no appeal. My parents and their neighbors had to carry the few pieces of household equipment they could salvage on their heads. We were reduced to the level of refugees from our traditional ancestral settlement to yet unknown destinations. My paternal grandmother, a widow, was unwell from lung cancer at this time of relocation. She joined us later but never recovered and two months later she died in July 1948, when my parents were busy constructing small dug and pole shelters for us to move into before they could start putting up permanent structures. The death of my grandmother at this time was a very big blow to me. I blamed the white farmer who had evicted us. At that early age, I grew up with a deep resentment of white settlers' faces. The image of one speaking to us seated on a horse haunted me for a long time.

I was the firstborn in my family and, according to Manyika tradition, the firstborn was often handed over to grandparents (the practice doesn't exist anymore). The idea behind it was to provide company to old grand-parents. So, I had everything I could wish for as a child because my grand-mother spoiled me. I was devastated when she passed on at an age when I needed her most. After having thought of myself as a single child, I rejoined my parents and my two younger brothers. Life was now different; I was no longer the sole focus of the family.

* * *

From my childhood until now, I have convinced myself that what I am today is what God planned for me to become. He fulfills His purpose, but without me being conscious of it, and life remains a miracle with its surprises.

Like any other child, I looked forward to the following day. And in-deed, the new day would faithfully be there with its surprises, good or bad, but all under God's control. Not knowing what the next day is going to be like is one of the best gifts God gives us day by day. We are reminded of our dependence on Him.

I did not know; when I was enjoying swimming in the pool in the river, that we would be forced out of Epiphany.

Little did I know that I would spend part of my childhood in Mata-beleland far away from Epiphany;

That one day I would be a priest, and that one day I would be a bishop;

That I would work as a priest in countries whose languages I did not understand or speak before;

That I would go to the United Kingdom where my childhood priest Father Henry Glover came from, to the country of white settlers who in-vaded my native country and named it Rhodesia after the name of their leader Rhodes;

That I would go to Sweden and meet my future wife from Germany;

That we would get married and settle in Germany;

That we would have three beautiful and intelligent daughters;

That we would go to the United States for further studies;

That we would come back to Zimbabwe, the country I was not allowed to set my foot in during Ian Smith's regime;

That we would be in Harare for quite a while before coming in a com-plete circle to my native Manicaland, the province where I was born, and then to be its Bishop.

The window is still opening. Where and when it will close, I do not know, neither do I have to know. After all, I am a sojourner in this world like everybody else. What I know to be there now is the guiding hand of God who will lead me to new horizons when his new window opens.

Even after the forced eviction, my life as a child was reasonably comfortable; we did not starve as so many did in Africa after World War II. We did not have everything that every child would want but there was enough to keep me and my five young brothers and our baby sister happy.

In 1983, forty-five years after our eviction, I took Rut and our two daughters to see my birthplace and refresh my childhood memories. We found neither a trace of our homestead nor the remains of a rusty skeleton of my beloved Benz—about which I tell more a bit later in this memoir. The entire Bakare clan's homestead had been razed to the ground and transformed into a tobacco field. All I could show them was tall savannah grass. My cherished childhood memories had evaporated and disappeared into thin air, but the negative experience I went through in the process of being evicted remains to this day. This bitter memory will be with me until the end of my life.

* * *

The bitterest part of my childhood story was when my mother told me that we were going to have to leave my life-size model Mercedes Benz behind. As a boy I had made this Benz with my own hands—it was my creation and the best thing I had ever possessed. The four wheels were made with different sizes of wire—thin wire in front, much thicker in the rear. The steering wheel was from a discarded bicycle. I had spent hours producing my Benz. It was hurtful for me to leave it behind, parked on the veranda. No one else understood the pain I went through because of the loss of my precious toy; the pain was beyond measure and the memory of abandoning my Benz haunted the rest of my childhood. I hated the white settlers for evicting us from our village and making me abandon my Benz. It's amazing how I have kept my anger against the settler regime for their being so inhuman to this day. But my tears were not compensated.

On the way to our designated destination, we children kept on asking our parents the same question: "When are we going to be there?" and "How long do we still have to walk?" Our parents just said, "Soon we will be there." After a day of trekking, we became tired, thirsty, and hungry. The second day, being the last lap of the journey, was gruesome and it seemed much longer for us children. While on the first day we were excited to run alongside our trotting animals, by the second day, we were exhausted and aching. This was my experience of invasion—as physical and psychological torture. The whole journey was about eighty kilometers—a long distance for children and for elders, carrying heavy loads on their heads.

My conclusion about the eviction from Epiphany is that an invader is a person whose brain is deformed. He or she has no feelings for their fellow beings; is heartless, and outright selfish. The memory of this horrible behavior by other human beings left a scar on my psyche. I developed resentment against the Native Commissioner in Rusape and his messengers who had brought the message of doom and darkness to Epiphany.

I grew up with rage against white settlers in Rhodesia, yet with a strong sense of hope and longing for the day when Africans would be able to live in a country where white settlers would behave more humanely than they did during the white colonial regime. But as a child I was helpless against the deprivation of the possession of my familiar childhood environment. I would no longer swim in the river or play with my beautiful Benz.

Our village priest, Father Glover, taught us the "Lord's Prayer" that says, "Our Father in heaven" cares for our daily needs. But for this evictor white farmer, God did not exist. His attitude toward us did not reflect that of a God-fearing individual. Insofar as he was concerned all people were not created equal.

A call to priesthood is to preach peace and justice, repentance, and forgiveness. I hold these to be the core values of the Gospel and I still believe that they are the basis of my call to the priesthood. A call to serve God's people regardless of who they are, black or white, regardless of their social status. God loves them to a be in good relationship with him and with each other. When I used to speak about the Rhodesians angrily, Rut would remind me to forget about the past behavior of the white settlers; they also need to be forgiven, she would say. My anger was always an expression of a wounded psyche in need of healing through forgiveness and reconciliation. Through Jesus' death on the Cross, we are forgiven and reconciled to God. But to this day in Zimbabwe, there is an absence of genuine repentance and forgiveness; tension and conflict remain the order of the day.

This brings me always back to the prophet Isaiah, who was called at a time when there was serious tension between Assyria and Judea. He said, "Here am I, send me." His call was to live his life reconciling the children of Israel to God, like his predecessors: Elijah, Elisha, and those who came after him, Jeremiah, Ezekiel, Amos, John the Baptist, to name but a few. They all suffered rejection. And Jesus' crucifixion on the Cross summed up a total rejection by his people to whom God sent him to preach repentance.

As one called to serve God's people, the death of Jesus on the cross reminds me that it is a call to a permanent ministry of reconciliation. This was Jesus' final act of love—shedding his blood to reconcile humanity still turns against turning. The cross was the ultimate end of his mission of reconciling rebellious humanity to God. After his resurrection, Jesus commissioned his disciple to carry on his mission of reconciliation. Through the ministry of reconciliation, enemies are brought to a good and loving relationship with each other.

CHAPTER THREE

Early Education

Cyrene Mission is an Anglican Boarding School founded in 1939, originally for boys. Cyrene is situated about twenty-five kilometers south of Bulawayo. It was founded by Canon Edward Paterson and became famous for its murals, and stone and wood carvings. Paintings of biblical and famous African stories covered the walls inside and outside the chapel. From Cyrene Mission Canon Paterson pioneered Mural Arts in Zimbabwe. The chapel paintings attracted tourists from as far away as the United States and it was my boarding school for my primary and secondary education.

In 1954, it was a great event when a group of American tourists came to our school. Among them was one black man who could not speak Ndebele or Shona, but only English. He wore black and white shoes that we called "shoeshine shoes," and a white hat to protect his face from the sun. He was of average height with a broad, smiling face. Our Principal asked him to sing for us and so we gathered outside the chapel to hear him. And the man who was introduced to us as Louis Armstrong started singing: "Down by the riverside...." and "Nobody knows the trouble I've seen ..." We were mesmerized by his voice. The two songs became hits for us. There was one student whose voice was like that of a frog; he could imitate Armstrong very well so we nicknamed him Armstrong. He became our Louis Armstrong and performed at our weekend concerts in the hall.

After Louis Armstrong finished singing, we asked him some questions about how he learned English so well. It was all new to us when explained that English is what American black people speak. As an adult, when I discovered that he came from New Orleans, I developed a liking for that city.

Years later my daughter Nyasha took me and my granddaughter Nomsa to New Orleans. I was so thrilled to walk in the same streets he had walked in. And the tradition of music, like in Armstrong's day, is still alive—musicians are found on many street corners blowing their trumpets.

When I was in New Orleans my mind went back to Cyrene and the memory was as alive as when I was a child. I cherish the memory of seeing Louis Armstrong standing in front of us, singing.

* * *

In 1959, two years after Ghana became independent of British rule, the Reverend Ndabaningi Sithole published his book, "African Nationalism." That small book sowed the seed of patriotism and nationalism among the youth of my generation. We became politically conscious of the ugly, oppressive system under which we lived. Even some liberal whites welcomed Sithole's treatise.

I had my copy which I read from cover to cover; it became my small bible. It gave me a sense of hope that Zimbabwe, like Ghana, might become free. My "childhood window" was opening wider to imagine a much bigger world beyond Rhodesia and to believe that what was happening elsewhere on the continent could also happen in Rhodesia. I asked myself why we in Rhodesia could not be like Ghana. What a dream or fantasy that was, but I and my schoolmates began to imagine what it would be like to move freely in the streets of our cities Bulawayo, Harare, Mutare, and Gweru, where now we encountered constant harassment from white teenage boys and law enforcement officials. The infamous apartheid law had become an accepted law in Rhodesia just as it was in South Africa. In department stores, like Meikles, Africans had to go to a window to pay for their goods, only whites could enter the store to shop in the usual way. Not only were blacks regarded as thieves, but the apartheid regime didn't want them near whites.

Bulawayo's Centenary Park was a popular place for children and it became a battlefield between black and white teenagers. Whenever we walked through the park, we saw to it that we had enough stones in our pockets, and so did the white boys. There was an unofficial liberation war between us. But the police always took the side of the whites.

But in March of 1957, the week Ghana attained self-rule on its way to becoming independent, the Reverend Ffrancon-Jones, our school's principal and rector, preached the sermon I have already mentioned that changed the course of my life with the text from Isaiah, Chapter 6, as the Lord says:

"Whom shall I send? And who shall go for us?" 'And I said, 'Here am I. 'Send me!'"

One day, Ffrancon-Jones called me to his office. I got there deadly scared, thinking that maybe I had done something wrong and was going to be severely reprimanded or expelled from school. Just a month before, my friend Hugh Bajila and I had fought the headmaster for punishing us because we came late to our evening study classes. We had been struggling with a diesel generator that would not start. This generator provided electricity for the whole mission, and had left everybody in the dark. We eventually got it going. The headmaster supervising evening classes still told us we deserved to be punished because we were late. Punished for making the engine start to provide light to the whole campus seemed unjust to us.

We had noticed that this headmaster had a racist attitude. As our punishment for being late to class, he told us to clear weeds on the paths and plant new blooms on a Saturday morning. When we didn't turn up, he came to haul us out of our dormitory in front of our classmates. He started hitting us, and Hugh and I began to hit him right back—like puppies attacking a Brahmin bull—and our fellow students cheered us on. We had put up with his racist remarks long enough, and the fight came out of all the accumulated anger against him.

So there we were, the following morning, being called to the principal's office. By that time, we regretted our behavior. Ffrancon-Jones asked us, "Tell me what is going on?" After hearing our side of the story, he simply said, "Go back to your class." We received a heroes' welcome from fellow students.

Hugh and I were the principal's favorites—we were the altar boys who stayed behind to clean up after the service when our fellow students were trying to beat each other out the chapel door like they were being chased by some wild animal.

So this time when I was called to the principal's office, and though I knew I had done nothing wrong, I was still frightened. The principal's office was intimidating enough, let alone with the fight with the headmaster still fairly recent. I humbly and politely entered the office almost with tears on my cheeks, and was shown to a chair. Ffrancon-Jones was not only the principal, he but was also the Rector of the Mission, chaplain of the school—and my Latin and Divinity teacher—with all the powers invested in those roles and titles. I sat there putting on a brave face ready to defend myself.

But his question came out of the blue. "Sebastian, what do you want to do when you finish school?" Before I could respond, he asked, "Have you ever thought about the vocation to the priesthood?" I told him that I had, but that I was too young to enter the seminary. To which he replied, "We will see as time goes on."

Two years later, when I was nineteen, Ffrancon-Jones was now in Lusaka, serving as the principal of Kabulonga Boys' School, which was also where St. John's Seminary was located. My friend Hugh and I were in Kabwe (Broken Hill) working for a building contractor who was wiring houses in a new residential area, a trade we had been taught at the mission school. I thought I was too young still to apply to seminary, so I was surprised when I got a letter inviting me to interview. It turned out Ffrancon-Jones had applied on my behalf. The interview was done by three priests, plus my old teacher Ffrancon-Jones, and I was admitted to seminary to start in January 1960.

I still have books that Father Ffrancon-Jones gave me for seminary on my bookshelves in Mutare. When I read some of his sermons, I realized what a powerful preacher he was, in a way that I didn't fully understand when I was a student.

CHAPTER FOUR

Training to Serve

An introduction to an understanding of my struggle with my life's mission is warranted here, though it will take me out of chronological order.

A call to priesthood is to preach peace and justice, repentance and forgiveness; I hold these to be the basic values of the Gospel and I still believe it is the basis of my call to the priesthood. A call to serve God's people regardless of whether they are black or white, regardless of their social status—they all belong to God who loves them and wants them to be in a good relationship with Him and with each other. But I came to seminary with a terrible scar from my childhood: the experience of eviction. Even today, I struggle with a spirit of antagonism toward white settlers.

When I used to speak about the Rhodesians angrily, my wife Rut would remind me to forget about the past behavior of the white settlers; that they also need to be forgiven, and that my anger was always an expression of a wounded psyche in need of healing through forgiveness and reconciliation. And, indeed, through Jesus' death on the cross, we are forgiven and reconciled to God. But in the absence of genuine repentance, forgiveness is not possible; tension and conflict remain the order of the day. This is what I saw—and still see—every day in Zimbabwe: serious tension between blacks and whites, between law enforcement agents and the public.

As one called to serve God's people, the death of Jesus on the cross reminds me that it is a call to a permanent ministry of reconciliation. This was Jesus' final act of love: shedding his blood in order to save humanity that turns its back on God. After his resurrection, Jesus commissioned his disciples to carry on his mission of reconciliation. And I am one of those who was called—sometimes gladly, sometimes reluctantly—for that mission.

All this, however, wasn't clear to me when I began seminary training in 1959 at only twenty years of age. Most of my classmates were grown men with families; some with children nearly my age. Though my parents had given me faith in God from childhood and I came to seminary with scriptural knowledge, I was lacking in theological basics.

Also, there was the question of ministerial formation. But that was supplied in seminary where we were involved in a rigorous program consisting of meditation and prayer. Our daily life was ordered as follows:

Half an hour meditation before Morning Prayer, followed by Eucharist;
Midday Prayer before lunch;
Evening Prayer before supper;
Compline before retiring for the night.

The day's program of contemplation, prayer and study started in the chapel where the cross reminded us of Jesus' mission of reconciliation and forgiveness. The altar was a place of sharing in His blood and body in memory of his death and passion until he comes again. The four walls of the chapel prevented us from outside distraction and created a still atmosphere for an ideal form of stillness.

I am indebted to the seminary community for having offered me this opportunity for formation and to become surer of my mission and closer to God. I thank God for St. John's Seminary, although it was a rigorous training. I was formed there and it is still forming me to be what I am today.

When I was at St. John's Seminary there were sixteen ordinands in all; six entered in the first year with me. Seminary wasn't easy for many of my fellow ordinands; two had to leave within a year for family reasons, while a third didn't feel called anymore. Sadly, three of those who were my classmates and made it through to ordination died after serving as priests for very short times. The regime was ruthless and life was very hard at that time.

Then, there were other aspects of my life that I now realize were so critical to my formation as a priest: my wife and my parents.

Every day, when I sit in our small chapel at home in Mutare, I feel consoled when I recall Rut's deep prayers as she sat next to me. She had the gift of saying the right words at the right time. Tom Shaw, the late Bishop of Massachusetts, who was a friar from the Society of St. John's Evangelist Community, in Cambridge, once remarked, "Rut's prayers are very deep and profound. Every time when it was her turn to do intercession, I felt uplifted by her prayers." Rut, as a fellow pilgrim, helped me to continue with my ministerial spiritual formation even long after I left seminary. For now, prayer remains my faithful partner on this journey until I join those who have gone before me. May God continue to grant both of them eternal peace.

When I look back, I admire my parents' faith in giving away their son to take up such a non-profitable profession. Priests were poorly paid though they were usually able to sustain their family from the small stipends they received. A call to serve people includes self-sacrifice but also to sacrifice the needs of one's family.

After my first year in seminary, and after we finished our ordination retreat led by Bishop Leslie Edward Straddling of Johannesburg, I started having second thoughts about ordination. Indeed, I had no desire to be ordained any more. I simply felt too young and inexperienced and the idea of standing in front of a congregation consisting of elders, professionals, people who knew more about life than I did, and trying to instruct them in Holy Scripture, terrified me. So, I went to see Archbishop Oliver Green-Wilkinson, the day before I was to be ordained to the diaconate. (In the Anglican church, aspirants are ordained as a deacon first, and then as priests.)

The Archbishop must have been stunned when I told him I had changed my mind about ordination, but if he was angry at me, he hid it. I think he realized I was in agony about this decision. Instead, he gave me a Biblical pep talk.

What the good man did was remind me of Samuel's boyhood when he was serving the priest Eli, and mistook God's call for the voice of his master. The third time, Samuel ran into Eli to ask what he needed, the priest told him, "If he calls you, you shall say, 'Speak, Lord for your servant is listening'" (1 Samuel 3:9). He also reminded me of Jeremiah who said, when the Lord called him, "Truly I do not know how to speak for I am only a boy," but the response was:

> Do not say, 'I am only a boy;
> for you shall go to all to whom I send you,
> and you shall speak whatever I command you.
> Do not be afraid of them,
> for I am with you to deliver you,

says the Lord. (Jeremiah 1:7-8)

I thought again about the sermon in the Chapel at St. Simon of Cyrene, "Your people are calling you." By then, I was totally disarmed, confused, feeling as though I was wandering through a strange landscape with great joys and terrors on all sides. The Archbishop did not give me a chance to respond. He was a prayerful person; he simply stood up, took my hand and led me to his chapel to pray. While he prayed, I knelt in silence beside him with my spirit in torment. But as I considered the examples of Samuel and Jeremiah as young men, probably younger than I was, my mind gradually eased. After a time of prayer and reflection in his chapel, we went back to his office and sat down—all in complete silence. He appeared to be very sad, perhaps he even internalized my spiritual agony.

I was now inclined to go forward with ordination, but I was also profoundly embarrassed and didn't know what to say to the good Archbishop. Hesitantly, I said to him, "Thank you for pulling me out and cleaning me from the morass of fear and doubt. I am willing to be ordained." He did not respond but kept on signing what appeared to be ordination papers, after which we shook hands and I left him.

The next day, December 8, 1961, the Archbishop asked, again, whether I was ready to be ordained, and I said: Yes. That was the day I was ordained as a deacon in God's One, Holy and Apostolic church. I was twenty-one years old.

Two years later, on December 17, 1963, I was ordained to the priesthood. The Cathedral of the Holy Cross in Lusaka had just been completed and this was the first grand event in the Diocese of Northern Rhodesia. We were honored by the presence of Sir Evelyn D. Hone, the last British Governor of Northern Rhodesia, a devout Anglican layman. He was accompanied by his regiment and the regiment band accompanied the service. It was an awesome event.

But for me the most important person in the congregation was my father who had travelled all the way from Southern Rhodesia in the company of my two brothers Cornelius and Hugh, and my cousin Victoria to witness this great event in my life. My father must have told his friends at home many stories in a variety of versions about his experience at my ordination. There were seven deacons ordained and two priests, and of the two priests, I was the first to be ordained in that brand new, august cathedral.

At my ordination to priesthood something extraordinary happened. My former headmaster who I had fought at school for punishing us was present and at the end of the service the two of us embraced. I had tears in my eyes, I was so overcome by the grace of God who made it possible for us to be reconciled to each other. He was a senior priest and realized what it meant for both of us to be called to the ordained ministry of reconciliation. At that moment of embracing, we felt the power of forgiveness and became free to relate to each other as friends and now as priests called to serve God's people. We both felt vindicated and forgiven.

It is a tradition in the high church that the newly ordained priest celebrates his or her first Eucharist in the presence of their families. My family was present in that service before they left for Rhodesia. It was a touching moment for me to administer communion, first to my father, brothers, and cousin before the congregation.

The following day my family left for Southern Rhodesia, while I left for my first posting as a curate at Msoro Mission in the Eastern Province of Northern Rhodesia. I was going to be priest to a people whose language I could not speak fluently. This was the first test of what it meant to serve God's people.

CHAPTER FIVE

First Parishes

O nly three days after I arrived as assistant priest at the Msoro Mission as a newly ordained priest, I was called to the hospital to attend to an old, dying lady. Seminary doesn't prepare you for the way being with a dying person focuses your faith and your hope in the resurrection of the dead. This first time was also terrifying for me as I had never been with a dying person before.

The old lady lay in a narrow bed, enclosed by a screen. No members of her family were there; the only people present at her deathbed were me and the nursing sister, who told me that she was old, although the date of her birth was not known. It's common among old people in the British colonies that the date of birth was never recorded and no birth certificate issued. The old lady looked so frail and withdrawn.

I officiated this rite with a trembling heart, feeling the momentousness of being the last person this lady would see before she passed on. It is the last sacred act we share with those leaving our earthly world. As my first time, I found the experience draining and not uplifting, because of all the emotions involved. At the same time, I felt humbled and privileged to be by the good woman's bedside as I signed the cross with holy oil on her forehead to complete the ritual.

Msoro Mission is near the Malawi border—then, it was the interior of the eastern province of Northern Rhodesia. It was a very rural area. Roads were bad, there was no telephone, mail was only delivered once a week during the dry season, and fortnightly during the rainy season when the roads weren't always passable. I was to minister to the Nsenga people whose language I couldn't speak well. The Mission, as it was called, was the first Anglican mission station in Northern Rhodesia founded by University Mission to Central Africa (UMCA) missionaries from London who arrived in the region from Nyasaland in 1911. I was the only African missionary out of seven British missionaries.

Here I was, in my mid-twenties, serving people who did not speak my mother tongue. Yet I was here to serve the people, visit the sick, administer the Sacrament of Holy Unction to the dying; be with those grieving for the loss of their loved ones. And I was also here to celebrate and share the joy with a couple at their wedding, and to share the joy with the parents at the christening of their infant.

The Msoro Mission Station is at the center of many small chapels in a district that extended more than 100 kilometers in either direction. To the West was Luangwa National Park, popular with tourists who came to view the game. It is home to lions, elephants, hippos, buffaloes, giraffes, crocodiles, all kinds of beautiful, wild birds—and tsetse flies that carried the dreaded sleeping sickness. Pastoral visits were done on bicycle, and it wasn't unusual to find an elephant blocking your path as you cycled through the game park. Because of the distances and the rough roads, pastoral visitations could take several weeks; the priest was always accompanied by a cook and two porters who brought along tins of beef, fish, mushroom, and tomato soup for sustenance, while parishioners added chicken and eggs to our meager meals when we visited them.

We sometimes slept in the animal viewing huts in the game park that were on stilts about ten-to-twelve meters high because of the lions that came out at night, prowling for their prey. One night I was terrified when two of the great lions rubbed against the posts holding the hut where I was sleeping. I thought they would bulldoze it down and I would become a good meal for them! I was often afraid on these treks—of being trampled by elephants, eaten by lions, or, more likely, contracting sleeping sickness. To ward off the tsetse flies—which I had never seen before this posting—I wore a plastic raincoat with a hood that covered most of my face, so I peered out through a tiny slit, trying to spy the elephants before they saw me as I rode along on my bicycle.

But by God's grace, I survived rampaging elephants, prowling lions, and tsetse flies, so I could live more fully into those words that kept haunting me: "Your people are calling you."

In 1964, while I was still at Msoro Mission, Northern Rhodesia achieved independence and became Zambia. Watching the people celebrate, I wished that my people in Southern Rhodesia would gain their independence; but that would still be twenty years in the future and my calling would take me far away from my homeland before it occurred.

I felt that my ministry at Msoro was what God wanted me to experience by serving people across cultural and different languages, yet I must admit when I returned to the Mission, I was grateful to have regular meals, instead of tinned food, a good shower, and a nice bed.

Our small missionary community consisted of eight staff members: four priests, one sister who was in charge of the hospital, a headmistress of the girls' school, a housekeeper, and a layman who later became a monk and moved on to St. Augustine's Mission, Penhalonga in Zimbabwe, where he died and is buried. Our priest-in-charge of Msoro Mission, our boss, Cyril Mudford fell in love at 75-years-of-age with Marjorie Bristow, our housekeeper, who was a year older than he was. They had the wedding of the century in our church, which has since become a cathedral. I remember how the schoolchildren asked us, Why isn't Marjorie pregnant? about a year after they were married. Perhaps they were thinking of the story of Abraham and Sarah; we priests could only chuckle and refrain from explaining things best left to their parents.

There was a lot I enjoyed about serving at Msoro Mission; there was much there that helped me form my call as a priest among the people. The only thing I didn't like was that that our domestic workers called me Mzungu, meaning European, because the food I was eating and the way I was being taken care of was the same as it was for the British missionaries. They also called me and the other missionaries Bwana, or boss. It took me a while, but I finally convinced them to call me, simply, Father Sebastian. Despite this, the people at Msoro never made me feel like a foreigner.

There was one very unexpected role I got to play, entirely by accident, just before I left Msoro to take up my new post as Rector of Cyprian's Parish in Mufulira, in the Copperbelt of Zambia. (The region was named after a big copper mine.) That was as a midwife; it was, in a way, the perfect close for my ministry at the Mission.

What happened was this: A week before I left Msoro to take up my new appointment as Rector of Cyprian's Parish in Mufulira, a message came through that a pregnant woman needed to be brought to the hospital to deliver her baby. I hurriedly jumped into the Mission's Land Rover, and drove the three miles to her village. She got into the flat bed of the truck so she could recline, and I drove her, as fast, yet as carefully as I could, on the very bumpy road back to the Mission and its hospital.

Suddenly, I heard "bang, bang, and bang" on the back window of the truck. I stopped, ran to the back of the truck, opened the tailgate, and realized I could see the baby's head showing. I thought of Blessed Mary and the Babe in the Manger in Bethlehem—Luke says only that the baby was born, wrapped in cloths, and placed in a manger—we're told nothing about whether the Blessed Mary was attended by midwives, or labored alone in that stable.

So here was this woman, stuck with a priest, trained in theology and ministry, but not trained as a midwife or doctor, who are the people one really wants when a child is coming into this world. Luckily, the mother was very calm, while it was all I could do to keep myself from fainting! A short time later, the baby was there, and his mother appeared to be doing well.

As I drove on to the hospital, I thought of the invisible hand of God doing and completing His work of creation while I was only a helpless assistant nurse in training. But I was there to take mother and baby to the mission hospital to get the after-birth care they needed. To be a midwife on a dusty road was something I never expected to encounter in my ministry, but it had happened to me, so very early on in my formation. It was like I was joining the mother at the deep end of the pool, and both of us had to find the strength—she to have her baby, me to get her to the hospital—to swim to the shallow end to serve the life of this newest of God's children. I can see the invisible hand of God performing and perfecting his work when I arrived at the Mission and administered the sacrament of Holy Unction to a dying woman, and in my witness to this baby's birth as I was about to leave the Mission. Those moments, so strangely framed at the beginning and the end of my first post, gave me a brand-new perspective of what the call to serve God's people is all about. And, as I've often been reminded over the years, responding to the call to serve God's people can lead priests into situations that we could never imagine. It's both wonderful, and it also reminds us that we are truly inadequate to do God's work.

When I was transferred to Mufulira in the Copperbelt region, I was again with people whose language, Bemba, I did not speak. (Bemba is spoken widely in Northern and Central Zambia.) It was the youth group in my congregation who taught me how to speak Bemba; indeed, I noticed that it was young people who were best at teaching me the local language when

I was in Zambia, and later, who helped me learn German when I went to that country. Also, because I grew up in a town, I have to admit I was happy to be away from the national park infested with tsetse flies and elephants.

I was sent to this parish because my predecessor was getting old and was no longer able to fulfill his pastoral responsibilities, and the parish was financially unable to meet its diocesan financial obligation. It was a bit daunting for a young priest with boundless energy, but little experience.

Unlike my bicycle experience at Msoro Mission, at St. Cyprian's I was given a Vespa scooter. I preferred my Vespa to a car for the practical reason that it was easier to park when I was out on my pastoral visits. Also, the majority of my congregants were miners, working in the big copper mines, and were often financially strapped, so I felt they would consider me to be one of them when I came to visit on my scooter. Some parishioners wanted their rector to drive an expensive car, like the pastors from smaller Pentecostal churches, but it didn't bother me. I was there to bring good news to the congregation and not to go around in a flashy-looking car.

I was young, unmarried, and had plenty of time to do parish work, and I got to know the miners well. The African miners in the Copperbelt were generally migrants from all over southern Africa. Though they were there for the long term, some of them still planned to return to their home countries upon retirement, meanwhile, St. Cyprian remained their spiritual home.

One of the main reasons causing the congregants to lose interest was the absence of parish activities such as the traditional mother's union, youth work, men's fellowship, such activities are the backbone of parish life, but at this parish, they were no longer in existence. My predecessor was a dear old man who was once a devoted priest but because of his age, was no longer able to run a parish.

When I took over as rector, it took me over a month to figure out where to start. I began with lapsed traditional activities. Members of the groups became my local missionaries who took their roles seriously by visiting people in their houses. I organized school teachers who helped me to run short seminars on leadership. The parish was galvanized and the groups worked together as members of one congregation. After a year we were able to meet our financial obligation to the diocese. During my second year the parish paid its diocesan assessment in advance for the whole year and in addition, also bought me a brand-new car—an Austin model—though I only got to drive it for three months before I left for England to pursue a graduate degree in education at the University of Birmingham.

My parish experience at St. Cyprians made me feel fulfilled. The good Lord had given me sufficient grace to work with members of the congregation who were committed to doing God's work, and I was able to leave the congregation in good financial standing.

CHAPTER SIX

A Window Opens to the Wider World

W hen I left Africa to pursue an education degree in Birmingham in 1966, I was again, as I had been as a child, an exile from my native land.

Ian Smith, the prime minister of Rhodesia, and a proponent of apartheid declared independence from Britain on November 11, 1965. England Prime Minister Harold Wilson had been trying to peacefully negotiate for a new nation that would result in majority rule and not hand all government power to the white oppressors. I was already involved in discussions with expatriates in Zambia about the new homeland we expected would come out of the talks between Smith and Wilson.

While I was at the Mindolo Ecumenical Foundation in Kitwe for a few weeks before I left for England, I got several messages from my father that he was constantly being harassed by the southern Rhodesian police. They were demanding that I pay the poll tax, even though I no longer lived in the country. I was outraged by this unlawful behavior. It also reminded me of the other inhumane acts by settlers in evicting us from our village when I was a child. I decided to burn my Rhodesian ID as a way to denounce the regime. It was an emotional response. Indeed, my good friend, Methodist Bishop Abel Muzorewa—who later became the Prime Minister of Zimbabwe during the transition from Rhodesia—warned me not to do it. But I went ahead and burned it, then sent the ashes in an envelope to William Harper, the Minister of Home Affairs in Salisbury (now Harare). The accompanying letter expressed my disgust with the police for demanding the poll tax from my father when I was no longer a resident. In return, I was declared *persona non grata* in my native country and my Rhodesian passport was revoked. Two months later on November, 11 1965, Ian Smith declared unilateral independence from Britain, which ignited the liberation struggle by Africans.

The thing I regret the most about my expulsion from my home country is that the last time I saw my father was at my ordination in 1963. He died in 1976, several years before I could return. Lord have mercy when we are treating each other like in this story.

* * *

Culture shock has accompanied me on almost every step of my journey. It was there during the first years of my life as an ordained minister to God's people when I had to adapt to a new language—and the tsetse flies—at Msoro Mission. St. Cyprian was another kind of culture shock—learning another new language and the culture of African miners. Now, in 1966, when I left Zambia to attend the University of Birmingham, I was in for an even bigger culture shock, trading the dry and hot sub-Saharan African climate for the wet and cold climate in the United Kingdom. I went from my hostel to the lecture theaters with my face almost completely covered, protecting myself from the bitterly cold and wet wind. My fingers were numb, so I bought myself a pipe and learned to smoke. I warmed my fingers by hold them around the pipe bowl and by the time I got to the lecture theater my fingers would be ready to take notes.

After my second year at the University of Birmingham, Patricia Page, an American missionary I had met in Zambia, wrote to tell me to expect a call from her friend Chris Howard. The call was an invitation to attend the World Council of Churches assembly meeting being held in Uppsala, Sweden in July 1968, to which I happily consented. I didn't even stop to think about how I, as a poor student, could pay for the trip and accommodations, but it turned out that Chris had agreed to underwrite my attendance as a steward. I was so stunned by her generosity I remember giving my thanks to her in the faintest of voices. I was thrilled to go and happy to give her a full report while I was at the conference and when I returned.

The WCC was founded in 1948 to work for ecumenism in the Christian church. The Assemblies were convened every few years—the 1968 Assembly was only the fourth since its founding. It was a momentous and violent time for the anti-war and civil rights movements. The Rev. Dr.

Martin Luther King, Jr. had been scheduled to give the Assembly's keynote address, but he had been assassinated in April. The writer James Baldwin gave a speech in his place, asking whether "there is left in Christian civilization the moral energy, the spiritual daring, to atone, to repent, to be born again." (This is not from my memory of the specific words Baldwin spoke, but from the WCC online archives, though I remember the thunderous applause from the assembly when he finished.) Baldwin also spoke on a panel at the Assembly, telling delegates that the Rev. King's assassination, the Vietnam war, South African apartheid were "crimes committed in the name of the Christian church." Baldwin warned that if the church could "not recover its Lord and Savior, Jesus Christ," by rediscovering "the meaning of what he said, what he meant, when he said, insofar as you've done it unto the least of these, you've done it unto me," then the church's structure "is doomed." (My thanks to the Presbyterian Historical Society, which has made the tape of Baldwin's panel address available online.)

The theme for the 1968 Uppsala Assembly was Revelations 21:5: "Behold, I make all things new." It marked the beginning of the ecumenical movement's involvement in many of the struggles for human rights around the world, including the anti-apartheid movement in South Africa.

For me, a student still in my twenties, there was something else happening I wasn't aware of, even taking into account my excitement at being at this international conference during my first visit to continental Europe. It was that I was about to meet my future wife.

There are many times we say things like "God has a plan," or "The Lord moves in mysterious ways," or "This is the Lord's doing," when what we mean is that something has happened that thwarts our earthly plans, and we are casting our disappointment and our doubt on God. But in the case of my meeting with Rut, my life partner, my friend, my wife for forty-eight years, I truly believe God was at work.

As these things often go, our first meeting was not propitious.

The stewards at the Assembly were mostly students from five continents who were recruited, as I was, to help serve in various functions during the meeting. There was an orientation meeting before the main business of the Assembly got underway. I was always very punctual, so I was the first steward to arrive in the hall where the orientation was being held, and so had an opportunity to talk to Philip Potter, the Methodist minister who later became the WCC's general secretary.

The hall began to fill up until most of the chairs were occupied, except one next to me. A beautiful young woman came in late and headed straight for that chair. I remember resenting that she chose that seat because I disapproved of people who weren't punctual. How God must have laughed at me for my petty resentment!

After the orientation session ended, we introduced ourselves, and there was another moment when I responded with some resentment to the silliest thing: Her name. In Birmingham, there was another Ruth from Copenhagen who always tried to sit next to me in the dining hall. That Ruth talked a lot and many students tried to avoid her; with my formal and polite upbringing I found I couldn't always do that. So the name already had bad associations for me.

During the course of the Assembly, which took place over more than two weeks, that feeling changed. For one thing, Rut, like me, didn't just talk for talk's sake; she responded mostly to inquiries from others. There was also something different about her from other young people, including myself: She was outstandingly generous.

The stewards had been given ten Swedish krona for pocket money. At the official opening service in the Uppsala Cathedral, I noticed that Rut gave all her pocket money to the offering for the Third World. I was embarrassed by her gesture and gave some money, but because I was from the Third World, I knew what it was like to go hungry, so I kept back some for myself.

At the same time, I was reminded of Jesus' response to the devil, "It is written: 'Man does not live by bread alone but on every word that comes from the mouth of God'" (Matthew 4:4). I was deeply impressed by her faith in God who provides us with our daily needs. I was a priest and here was a layperson who had a heart for the poor, particularly widows and orphans in the third world. She demonstrated her faith in action.

Of course, I also belonged to a people who lived in a continent of scarcity and sometimes extreme poverty compared to her affluent society. Still, I did not put all my faith in works in the same way as Rut demonstrated her faith through that simple, but meaningful donation.

We walked back together to our residence hall after the service in a downpour. Rut had a small umbrella, which she wouldn't share. How odd that must have looked. Here, this young, German woman had just given her last coin to the poor who she did not know, yet she wouldn't share her umbrella with the African man with whom she was becoming acquainted.

But I could tell something else was going on. To share her small umbrella with me meant walking very closely together, perhaps even touching, and, as a moral young woman of another time, that was against her principles. Oddly, though I was drenched from our walk through the rain, I also respected her for the way she held to her principles.

Years later, now as husband and wife, Rut would tease me with the parable of the poor widow who gave all she had and the Pharisees who believed in hoarding their money for the future.

The next day, with the money that I had held back from the offering plate, I went downtown and bought my own umbrella, twice the size of hers, so if need be, I could share it with her without walking too close. When I managed to buy my own the umbrella issue was solved; we became inseparable friends during the Assembly.

One of the things that was interesting about both me and Rut was, despite our youth, we had an understanding of things happening in the world beyond the boundaries of our home countries or continents. I credit my father with that; he always told me there was a bigger world beyond Rhodesia.

An experience I remember most clearly sharing with Rut was a series of Pete Seeger concerts held during the Assembly. His music spoke not only to the students, but also to all the anti-war activists. Seeger's music, the words of his songs, "Where have all the flowers gone?" "We shall overcome," with more than 700 delegates from all over the world singing along gave us—gave me—such inspiration.

Indeed, the students who were serving as stewards demonstrated in the streets of Uppsala to bring awareness to the people about poverty, war and injustice. Some of the students were even arrested, though they weren't held for long.

In Uppsala, I was privileged to meet Christians from all over the world and also from my country, as the Zimbabwe Council of Churches was represented by its founder, Bishop Kenneth Skelton of the Diocese of Matabeleland who was accompanied by the Reverend H. Chikomo, the ZCC's General Secretary, and Mr. J. Mfula, Assistant Director from Mindolo Ecumenical Foundation, Zambia. It was a momentous moment for me to meet these honorable gentlemen from Rhodesia, a country that had taken away my birthright and prohibited me from setting foot on my native soil. Bishop Skelton knew about my situation and encouraged me to carry on with my studies. He assured me that Rhodesia would be free, whether Ian Smith liked it or not. How prophetic he was!

Bishop Skelton was disappointed about the lack of support from other African churchmen; how sad it was that this Bishop was the only voice in the Anglican Church in Rhodesia who condemned discriminatory laws passed by an illegal regime. I had hoped that one day after Independence I would serve under his leadership, but that was not to be. His preaching that resistance to tyranny and racism was a Christian duty was a thorn in the side of Ian Smith. He was forced to resign because he stood for peace and justice which was perceived as bad news by the racist regime. He returned to England where he served in the church until his retirement. (Bishop Skelton died in 2003.)

When I went back to Birmingham after Uppsala I had a different view, a wider and more ecumenical view, of the church and the world. I had been raised in the High Anglican tradition and I didn't have an understanding of other denominations, but now I came to appreciate the teachings of other churches. Years later, when I was doing graduate theological work at the Graduate Theological Union in Berkeley, I had the good fortune to have excellent teachers from outside the Anglican tradition. I especially remember Robert MacAfee Brown, whose systematic theology lectures on liberation theology and the spiritual prophetic were not only learned, but inspiring.

And when it came time for me to write my thesis at the Graduate Theological Union, in Berkeley, California, I asked Professor Herman Waetjen, a Presbyterian, to be my advisor, not least because the Episcopalian professors weren't interested in my proposed topic: A Theology of Land in Zimbabwe. Professor Waetjen, on the other hand, was very encouraging and supportive as I did the hard work of a doctoral thesis.

When the Assembly was over, it was also time to say goodbye to the beautiful German woman with whom I had become such good friends, so quickly. To me, Rut was no longer just a white person but a pure human being free from any consciousness about differences in skin color. Rut was very vocal about her solidarity with the Third World delegates present at the Assembly, and there were others like her, with whom we formed a commonwealth fellowship of Christian friends.

I returned to Birmingham, and Rut to Germany. But that was not an ending, it was a beginning.

CHAPTER SEVEN

Christmas in Germany

This next chapter is about what happens when two people from entirely different parts of the world meet and decide that the other is the person they want to spend the rest of their life with.

But if you are looking for the expected trappings of romance, you will need to look elsewhere. African men, as a rule, hold their feelings close. And those many of us who lived through hard times, wars, and oppression learned to hold our feelings even closer. So, I will stick mostly to the facts, and let others fill in the emotions.

Also, I was a young priest when I met Rut in Uppsala at the World Council of Churches conference. And I could imagine what my Bishop would think—did he commend my further education in England so that I could gallivant around with beautiful young women? Or did he expect me to attend to my studies so I could return and serve Africa's young people?

It is a common practice in Germany for families to invite people who are likely to be alone to join them during the festive season and, in particular, on Christmas. And grown children are invited to bring along their friends who cannot be with their families. So it wasn't that surprising that in November of 1968, I received a letter from Rut that read: "Why don't you come to Germany for Christmas since you don't have a family in the United Kingdom?" She continued, "You should come and experience something different."

I was reluctant to go, mostly because I could not speak German. But, on second thought, I decided to accept. I remember telling my English friends in the hostel where we lived that I was going to Germany for

Christmas and one young lady from Sheffield said to me, "Do you want to go to West Germany and miss the Queen's speech on Christmas Day?" Of course, I had heard the Queen's Christmas speech every year as the BBC broadcast it throughout the British Empire. I told her that I was from Rhodesia, an oppressed British Colony, and my interest in her speech was zero.

My Christmas trip included a ferry ride that, given the winter weather, was anything but smooth. But eventually, I arrived in Gelsenkirchen, a city whose main industry was coal mining, in the North Rhine-Westphalia, where I was warmly greeted by Rut's parents, Hans Büchsel, a Lutheran pastor, and his wife Magdalena.

I also discovered that, because Germany's African colonies had been taken away by the Allies after World War I, Africans were a rare species in the country, unlike in the United Kingdom.

In Gelsenkirchen, I was always amazed at how people would stare at me. Whenever I walked by or entered a shop, I could see around me how Gelsenkircheners would regard me with curious and nervous eyes. And when I would greet them in German with a "*Guten morgen*," (good morning), they would look embarrassed and sheepish. It reminded me of a pastoral visit to the Angoni villages in Zambia with a white missionary colleague–how children in the villages would touch him and compare their black hands to his white ones. He was too tall for them to touch his hair, but they would have if they could. I was personally embarrassed at their curiosity and my colleague was not a fan of being swarmed all over by the children.

* * *

When I visited Rut and her family that Christmas, I wasn't aware that there was anything special happening between us. One thing I always knew, however, was that we were able to have meaningful theological discussions because we were both educated in theology.

I remember small things about that first Christmas in Germany—like the friends who came from Amsterdam on Christmas Day and the snowball fight we had in the fresh snow. But Rut and I were still just good friends. Maybe something was happening I was unaware of, but the idea of falling in love was so remote as to be impossible.

Then there were other barriers that I had to wrestle with, that went beyond the most obvious ones; like that I didn't speak German and also, apartheid at home. Whites and blacks were enemies in Rhodesia. Getting beyond that to think about proposing to a beautiful white woman? Quite a leap.

But, as always, God had a plan. And both Rut and I trusted in God's plan for us.

* * *

When I returned to England to complete my studies at the West Hill College of Education, Rut and I began to write to each other. When she was due to visit a friend in Hereford, I invited her to come up to Birmingham and she accepted.

When she came for a weekend in Birmingham, I think we both knew that we had committed to each other. I cannot now remember who brought up the idea of engagement, but one of the issues was that I was going to have to return to Zambia to serve the church that sponsored me to study in Britain. So that put some pressure on us to make decisions about our lives together. We were so young, and yet, we were already so serious about this!

When I finished my studies in Birmingham, on my way back to Zambia, I stopped over in Gelsenkirchen to formally propose marriage. Her father invited a few of his Lutheran pastor colleagues and a few church elders and their spouses to celebrate our engagement. At our *polterabend*—a German ritual performed the evening of the engagement—friends brought glasses, plates, and other household items and broke them in front of everybody. This custom is intended to bring the couple good luck— "*Scherben bringen Glück*" (shards bring luck). (Jewish readers will recognize this as similar to the custom of breaking a glass at the wedding.) Rut and I wore our engagement rings engraved with our names that her father had ordered for us before the *polterabend*. The evening included several very touching speeches from friends who wished us well.

It would be a year before Rut and I were married in a civil ceremony in Zambia, and three years before we would have our church wedding in her father's parish in Gelsenkirchen. Sadly, I left my fiancée two days after our engagement for Jerusalem with a brief stopover in Rome on my way to Zambia. What I couldn't know at that time was that I would eventually work as pastor in a nearby parish to my father-in-law's parish in Gelsenkirchen where we were married. With God all things are possible.

* * *

39

After our engagement, I left for Rome to stay overnight at the Anglican Center. Because I was in the Eternal City for such a short time, the next morning I ran out without breakfast, wanting to see as much of Rome as I could before my flight. At midday, I sat down to lunch at a restaurant around the Vatican Square—I had a full view of the veranda where the Pope, on solemn days like Easter and Christmas, pronounces his blessing: "Orbis et Urbi." It was hot and being famished and thirsty, without thinking, I ordered a liter of red wine. (In my defense, I was accustomed to the British measurement system of pints and I thought a liter was the equivalent.) Consequently, I became drunk. Cars and buses on the streets appeared to be running upside down. I was unable to stand. I must have sat there for an hour. I thought about my fiancée, what she would make of me if she knew that I was drunk in front of Orbis et Urbi. When I finally sobered up a bit, I walked quickly back to the Anglican Center to pack my bags and leave for the airport. When I got there, I discovered my flight to Jerusalem had left an hour before. I felt incredibly stupid.

But I was in Italy—and wearing a clerical collar. One of the flight attendants said, "Padre, wait, we will get a place for you on a flight going to Tel Aviv." And within an hour, I was flying on Trans American Airlines to Israel.

By the time I arrived in Tel Aviv, it was already evening and the Sabbath had started. My host thought I wasn't coming and left for Jerusalem. I finally found a taxi driver—not easy to do on the Sabbath—and made my way to Tel Aviv.

On the drive from Tel Aviv to Jerusalem, I was excited to see The Holy City, Zion the City of God. I kept thinking of the hymn: "Jerusalem, my happy home/When shall I see you." My host, Naim Atteek, a Palestinian priest, was a Canon of St. George's Cathedral. Years later, he would be at the Graduate Theological Union in Berkeley where I also would study.

Canon Ateek took me around the old part of Jerusalem. I remember so well my first glimpse of the Western Wall, the remains of the wall that Herod erected surrounding the Temple. I saw religious Jews knocking on the Wall as they prayed for the Messiah to come. Of course, being Christian, I thought, they are two thousand years late! We also toured those sites of such significance to Christianity: the Garden of Gethsemane, the Place of the Crucifixion, and the Sepulcher, where Jesus was buried.

On the second, day I was in Jerusalem, I met an African-American couple who were traveling with their teenage daughter, and they invited me to tour with them. I was glad to accept their generosity because my small pocket money wouldn't allow travel outside of Jerusalem. We went in their hired car north to Galilee, the Sea of Galilee, and Capernaum, and on to Nazareth and Samaria.

In Nazareth-Cana of Galilee, we met a Franciscan friar who invited us to his community to taste wine that was made in the same tradition as the wine that Jesus made from water at the Wedding of Cana. I have to admit, the wine was very good—maybe because it truly was the original wine!

The next day we went to the Dead Sea and visited the Qumran Caves. On our way back to Jerusalem we stopped in Jericho and Bethany. One thing I noticed was that the road from Qumran to Jericho was very lonely. It reminded me of the story of the Good Samaritan and the man who was robbed and left for dead by some robbers on the road.

I was humbled by the generosity of my new friends who had made it possible for me to see some of the places far away from Jerusalem. When they left me in the city, they wished me well in my ministry. Unfortunately, I didn't take down their names so that I could keep in contact. But when I got home, I often preached about their generosity. I would note that very few Africans would give a stranger a free ride for hundreds of kilometers, but this couple knew how to practice loving one's neighbor.

The next day I attended Sunday mass at St. George's Cathedral, truly an inspiration. The liturgy of the Eucharist was the same as in the rest of the Anglican Communion, yet here I was in the very city where it all began, two thousand years ago, in the "upper room," and where Jesus was rejected and ultimately crucified—Zion, City of God, Jerusalem, the epicenter of Christianity.

* * *

When I arrived back in Zambia, I was admitted to hospital suffering from pneumonia that I had contracted in Gilwell Park in Essex, during a training course for scout commissioners, which the diocese wanted me to fulfill as the Scout Movement was popular with the youth of the time. East Anglia was flooded and we did our training under terrible wet and cold conditions. We trudged about in water about a foot high every day and slept in raised, stilted huts—not good for a young man from sub-Saharan Africa. Though the Englishmen attending the course enjoyed it, it put me off the Scout Movement entirely, and I never made use of my certificate as a commissioner.

All the time I traveled from England to Zambia I felt weak, but I thought it was just the excitement and fatigue of travel, so I was surprised when the doctor told me I had pneumonia. While I was in my sickbed, I had a surprise visit from Bishop Kenneth Skelton from the Diocese of Matabeleland. He had driven from Ndola to Kitwe, where he was attending the Provincial Synod. It was so nice of him to be so concerned about me. He was very keen for me to return home but I reminded him that I was *persona non grata* in Rhodesia. (Years later, my good Bishop Skelton was deported from Rhodesia because he became unbearable to the racist regime of Ian Smith.)

My fiancée joined me in Zambia after a year of not seeing each other. I was based at Mindolo Ecumenical Foundation where I operated as secretary for Anglican schools in the country. This job enabled me to travel widely in Zambia where there were Anglican Church schools.

* * *

Rut was very much aware that Rhodesia was a country that, like South Africa, practiced apartheid. When she came to join me in Zambia, though I couldn't return to Rhodesia, Rut felt that being so very nearby, she couldn't return to Germany without seeing the people who were to be her in-laws. Taking a leaf from her biblical name, "your people will be my people, where you go, I will go and where you stay, and your God will be my God" (Ruth 1:16). This was a statement expressing her faith and courage.

Sometimes, I wondered what Rut's friends thought of her engagement to an African, and, even more, her intention to settle in then-apartheid Rhodesia. Years after we were married, and I was about to receive my graduate degree from the Graduate Theological Union in Berkeley, I told a classmate that we would be going back to Zimbabwe soon after graduation. She said, "Sebastian, you should get a job here in California or elsewhere in the United States. Do you want to take your wife and your daughters to Africa—a continent where there is hunger and poverty, tribal wars and diseases?" I ignored her, but she said out loud what others likely thought.

In the Bible, Ruth's love and care for her mother-in-law Naomi demonstrated her courage by breaking the political, religious, and racial divide between the two nations. Naomi probably died before Ruth who also followed her and was buried in Judah alongside Naomi according to her wish: "Where you die, I will die, and there I will be buried." Care, commitment, selflessness, courage, trust, faith, hope were as true of my Rut as they were of her biblical namesake.

Not only did the biblical Ruth devote her life to the caregiving of her mother-in-law Naomi, but she was also a caregiver to the wider community in Bethlehem-Judah. As was my Rut. My wife was committed to the care of widows, orphans, poor and hungry children in Mutare, founding a Trust that still carries on her work. I am grateful to friends overseas who send the trust donations to sustain its work.

The Book of Ruth has some unique aspects to its story, including some special theological elements that encompass a call, or vocation to serve God's people. Diaconal services, dedication, commitment, compassion, self-denial—all these elements have to do with the vocation to serve God. My life companion Rut embodied the spirit of the story. She grew up in a lovely family and her father was the eighth generation in the ordained Lutheran ministry and held deeply Christian values. Theology and politics were always topics of conversation in her home; I sensed it that first Christmas, even though I couldn't speak German. During that very first visit and thereafter Rut and I always talked about racism in Rhodesia and South Africa and the wars of liberation on the African continent.

Rut took advantage of Zambia's proximity to Rhodesia to cross the Zambezi River and travel to meet my family—a courageous move on her part as the divisions between black and white were very strong at that time. On the bus from Lusaka to Salisbury, she was the only white passenger on the coach—a new experience for her. Luckily, that coach didn't allow dogs, chickens and goats, like some other parts of Africa, which would have been an extra shock! At the Chirundu border post, the white immigration officer asked her to fill in the form where it asked where she was staying. She wrote: "Salisbury Hotel," a fictional hotel. But because she was white, nobody asked further questions. (I remained back in Mindolo; very anxious about her journey.)

On Rut's arrival in Salisbury, she was met by my brother Cornelius and his daughter Rosemary and was taken to a hotel then known as Federal Hotel which was multiracial in that people of all races—except white people—could stay and meet without being harassed by law enforcement agents. My niece Rosemary stayed with her in the same room overnight—an illegal act at that time as black and white were not allowed to stay in the same hotel room. Meanwhile, my parents arrived from Rusape and stayed at my brother's house for the night.

The account of her adventure in Rhodesia came from Rut when she returned. Before cell phones, there was very little communication when one was traveling.

The day after Rut arrived, she and Rosemary went to meet my parents, two brothers, and their wives and go about twenty kilometers away from Harare to picnic at Chivero Dam. The dam supplies the greater Harare area with water and has lodges and big picnic areas. Most shocking to Rut was that she was told by an African waiter that she couldn't use the toilet, because that was for whites. Because she was in the company of black people, she had to go in the bush. In a sense, she was no longer white but black. My father was disgusted and angry when he saw how his soon-to-be daughter-in-law was denied permission to use the white lady's toilet. He started cursing Ian Smith and his discriminatory laws—cursing "heaven and earth" as we say in Shona.

My father said, "This is the true and ugly face of racial discrimination enforced by blacks on behalf of the white with a pathological short circuit in their psyche." (I am translating literally from Shona.) The majority of blacks in Rhodesia had accepted the status quo of white racism and this was Rut's first encounter with that reality.

On another day, they drove out to the countryside to Dendenyore, with Rut ducking down when there was concern that the police might see her because whites were not allowed to go out to rural areas without permission. People in Dendenyore didn't have flush toilets as in Harare, but Blair toilets in an outhouse. Observing the poverty of black people in the rural areas and the affluence of whites in the cities, made Rut the ardent liberation activist she became when we were in Germany, where our rectory became a place for Zimbabweans to stay when they were on fundraising trips for the liberation movement.

* * *

Though I had given my best to serve the good people of Zambia, the road could be lonely and dangerous. I remember a time when I encountered lions lying on the road, blocking it while they basked and enjoyed themselves in the sunshine. It was not like seeing them in the game park—it was scary, especially as I was alone. Some of the roads to isolated schools were very lonely; one could drive for miles without seeing a single soul on the road. I was always fearful that I would get a flat tire and be stranded. I was always happy when I returned safely to the Mindolo Ecumenical Foundation offices. Back to civilization as it were.

Also, there was an additional problem with my relationship with Zambian priests. They thought that my position on the Christian Education team which later included a lecturer position at St. John's Seminary in Lusaka, should have gone to a Zambian priest, though none of them at the time had the qualifications for the job.

The job itself was rewarding, but also demanding, as I had to cover all the church schools in the country and make plans for and teach my seminary classes.

That's when Rut suggested that I apply for a teaching job in Germany, an idea that was most welcomed by my father-in-law. I was successful in my application for a work permit, but now the question was, what to do about traveling to West Germany? And, more important, what to do about our engagement.

CHAPTER EIGHT

Two Weddings and Return to Germany

Rut and I could have stayed in Africa. Rut was prepared to teach and had been offered a position in Kitwe. We also could have gone to Namibia where Bishop Colin Winter, the Anglican Diocesan Bishop, whom we got to know while he was on sabbatical in England, was keen to have us in his diocese. Having experienced discrimination from fellow Africans in Zambia, I was reluctant to go to another African country to face similar problems. But now, with the work permit in hand, we felt secure to go to Germany, join Rut's family, and forget about Africa for now. Of course, I had to learn German to teach comparative religion in Versmold, where I had secured a position, but I already spoke several languages, so I was sure I could do it.

What we discovered, though, was that if we wanted to get married in Germany, I would have to supply my birth certificate, which the Rhodesian government was not about to give me. I had a special passport from England, as I was living in exile from Rhodesia. We were advised to have a civil marriage first in Zambia and then follow up with a church wedding when we went to Germany.

I discovered that the Kitwe marriage registrar was a member of my congregation in Mufulira and he was so happy to perform the civil marriage ritual for his former Rector. Ezekiel and Ella Makunike, who lived with us on the same campus at Mindolo, were our marriage witnesses. On the evening of our civil marriage, we had a small party with a few friends.

It was also another evening of goodbyes, as we were leaving the following morning for Germany.

With the civil marriage certificate in our hands, my father-in-law took over the entire wedding arrangements. On July 28, 1971, the ceremony took place in his church in Gelsenkirchen-Rotthausen and was conducted by the President of Westphalia, Dr. Hans Timme, assisted by my friend, the Rev. Beaumont Stevenson, an Anglican priest from Oxford. He was the only person from my circle of friends, as my family and other relatives were not able to get visas to attend.

It was an ecumenical ceremony, which had never taken place before in this Lutheran congregation. A large number of curious people came to see their pastor's daughter getting married to an African.

* * *

A year after we were married, our eldest daughter, Nyasha was born. Like many first-borns, she picked up adult language quickly. She was also a quiet and observant child—Tinao, the middle daughter born about three years later, was the super-active one.

Tinao's active disposition proved nearly fatal when we were in Milan on a vacation trip to Italy when she was about four. We visited the Milan Cathedral which I was especially interested to see because a famous African church father, Augustine of Hippo, was baptized there by immersion. It is said that when Augustine emerged from the font, he started singing the *Te deum laudamus*: "We praise you O Lord and magnify your name." Because the police warned us that thieves were targeting cars, Rut stayed behind in the car and I took the two girls to see the famous cathedral.

The view from the domed roof has a panoramic view of the city, so, of course, we ascended. While I admired the view of Milan, Tinao, as usual, was jumping all about. Suddenly, she slipped and fell, sliding down a set of steep stairs. By God's providence, a German couple nearby grabbed her by the hand and stopped her fall. I almost fell myself as my knees had turned to jelly. In all these years, I have never forgotten that moment.

* * *

The first time I was in the United States I had moved on from teaching to be Rector of a parish in Schalke. I was traveling with a program from the continuing education college from Westphalia that was organized to visit several theological institutions in America. There were twenty pastors on the study tour. We started in Los Angeles where we visited Claremont Graduate School of Theology and Fuller Seminary, then we flew north to San Francisco to the Graduate Theological Union in Berkeley, a consortium of eleven theological schools. Berkeley was a very valuable exposure for us all. We had discussions with world-renowned theologians like Robert McAfee Brown, Massey Shepherd, and Frederick Borsch, later to be the Episcopal Bishop of Los Angeles.

During this brief visit to Berkeley, I met Professor Sam Garrett at the Church Divinity School of the Pacific (CDSP), an Episcopal seminary. We discovered that we had a common friend, Mrs. Ruth Harris, who was a missionary in Zambia, working for the World Council of Churches at the Mindolo Ecumenical Foundation. He asked me whether I was willing to come to the United States to do a Master's in theology. I told him that I did not have the funds to pursue further studies. And, in addition to that, I was married with two daughters and we were very happy in the parish. He told me that CDSP could take care of the funds. When we left Berkeley two days later, I thought that would be the last time I would be there. Of course, one day, I did indeed return to Berkeley with my family.

The tour went on to New York where we visited General Theological Seminary, the oldest Episcopal seminary in the United States, and Union Theological Seminary, where we had a fascinating theological discussion with Professor James Cone, on Black American Theology. My German colleagues were surprised to discover that Cone had written his doctorate on Karl Bath and they were extra attentive to him. On our final leg, we came back to Los Angeles, where we did a little touring about, including visiting Pasadena, Hollywood, and Beverly Hills.

It was a wonderful trip, though spoiled somewhat when my wallet was stolen, including all my money and ID, when I went into the Los Angeles post office to buy stamps.

* * *

After my father died in 1976, I was very concerned about my mother, who I hadn't seen in years. Rut and I were also worried that she would die before the country was liberated from the colonial regime and we could return.

When Ian Smith declared Rhodesia's unilateral independence against Britain in 1965, the Western countries withdrew their embassies in Rhodesia leaving only small consulates behind which weren't very helpful when it came to getting a visa. My mother attempted several times to apply for a visa and the German consulate flatly refused to handle her application, citing the lack of diplomatic relations between Rhodesia and the Federal Republic of Germany. Also, it was said that Germany considered Rhodesian Africans a risk. This last reason was unacceptable to Rut—surely her mother-in-law, a woman well into her sixties was a risk to no one. Through Rut's efforts, the German Minister of Foreign Affairs, H.-D. Genscher, not only responded positively to her letter, he also sent a directive to the consulate in Rhodesia that Mrs. Eunice Bakare should be granted a visa. There was great jubilation in the family upon receiving the good news. It was the first plane trip for my mother.

When I met my mother at the airport, after eighteen years of separation, I was shocked to see how old she looked. And now, she saw her son grown-up and the father of her grandchildren.

Everything was new and strange for her. She told us how she met a white passenger who helped her with her luggage. For her, coming from Rhodesia where white men treated African women without respect, this was a confusing experience. Then, on the plane, white women helped her with her seat and served her meals—another thing totally outside her experience in apartheid Rhodesia.

In Germany, it was hard for my mother to figure out how people could live in a big city without any fields. Even city dwellers in Zimbabwe grew crops like maize in plots next to their houses. And fields surround Zimbabwean cities. So, my mother kept asking: Where are the fields?

I remember Rut explaining to her that people in Gelsenkirchen worked in office buildings, while the fields for crops were in other areas. My mother took many pictures home with her to show friends and relatives this strange German city, and especially, snow, which many of her countrymen had never seen.

Rut brought my mother with her to a parish women's group that met every Wednesday for prayers and to celebrate their life together. My mother was the only black woman there and when she asked why, and her question was translated for the group, they burst into laughter.

Then, my mother, with Rut translating, told the assembled women's prayer group about the Mother's Union. In Rhodesia, during the Liberation War, the Mother's Union met in private homes and in churches where one could trust there were no informers. The Mother's Union was there to support each other and their families while they were at war with Ian Smith's soldiers. Despite the language barrier, a true spiritual bond was formed between my mother and the women's prayer group.

CHAPTER NINE

My First Vote

While my mother was visiting, momentous things were happening in Zimbabwe: they were preparing for the first general elections that would lead to independence for my native land. I left my mother in Rut's good company to fly home to vote, at age forty, for the first time in my life.

It was now 1980. I had waited so many years for this and I felt I couldn't miss the historical event. Some of my compatriots in the Diaspora did not bother to go home to cast their votes because they had lost hope for a free Zimbabwe. Some parishioners in Gelsenkirchen could not understand why I should travel that far just to cast a vote. They didn't understand that Africans weren't eligible to participate in elections because of discriminatory laws, and that they had no right even to live in a place of their choice. An election victory would give Africans the right to have a government of their own choice.

Rhodesia was still under United Nations sanctions and there weren't many airlines flying into the country, so I had to fly home from Brussels through Brazzaville. Two days after my arrival in Salisbury, my brother's son-in-law dragged me to see Bishop John Paul Burrough. The Bishop and I had exchanged some nasty correspondence about his racist attitudes, and he was the last person I wanted to see on this occasion, but I gave in to his insistence. We had no appointment and the receptionist tried to turn us away, but when he heard my name, Bishop Burrough came out and embraced me as though we were close friends. When we were alone, the bishop began our conversation by telling me he had just arrived from St. Faith-Rusape, my home district. On his way to Salisbury, he told me that he had given a lift to two young white men. And, seemingly without thinking who he was talking to, he said he told those men to go and join the Rhodesian Army and finish off those who were fighting against the government.

I was prepared to be reconciled with the bishop until he said this. I was so offended at his telling me how he encouraged the young white men to go and kill what he called "those Africans in the bush," as though he was not talking about my neighbors and kin. I stood up and bade him goodbye. I left his office wishing I could cast one hundred votes against the white regime at the polling station the following day, to be rid of people like him.

On February 14, 1980, I got up early in the morning to be among the first to cast my vote against Ian Smith. By noon, I was at the airport on my way back to West Germany, excited at exercising what should be the right of all citizens. On April 4, 1980, the results were announced: Robert Mugabe's Zimbabwe African National Union party (ZANU) had won.

Friends streamed into our big rectory lounge to congratulate us and celebrate the big victory. They came from our parish and from neighboring towns—Mulheim, Duisburg, Essen, Oberhausen, Bochum, Dortmund. Dr. M. Braun, a great liberation supporter, had passed the word to all solidarity friends in the area to converge at the Bakare home in Gelsenkirchen Schalke. It was a joyful occasion. We were celebrating the death of an oppressive regime and at the same time rejoicing at the birth of a new nation.

It seemed like everyone brought flowers as a celebratory gift. My mother, who was still visiting, was almost covered in flowers where she sat on the sofa. It was very odd for her, as she was only accustomed to seeing them at funerals, where they are thrown in the grave to bid farewell to the departed. She was overcome to see many of our friends celebrating our independence; all she could say in Shona was *tatenda*, which means thank you. Though she also said she was so happy to see Robert Mugabe's face for the first time on TV. I was overjoyed that I had gone all the way to Rhodesia to cast my vote, and that it had not been in vain.

* * *

Around this time, I received a letter from the good Professor Sam Garrett, telling me that the Mercer Foundation had agreed to offer me a scholarship to do a master's degree in theology at the Graduate Theological Union in Berkeley. The scholarship came as a big surprise—I had given up all hopes to do further theological studies.

But there were hurdles to overcome before I could go abroad to study.

Although I had been awarded a scholarship, I still had to get a recommendation from my home diocesan bishop who had to guarantee that I could get a job in the diocese after graduation. The bishop in question was the very same Paul Burrough who had so offended me with his racist comments on the occasion of the historic vote! But if I wanted that scholarship, I would have to write to him to request his endorsement. To my surprise, he responded positively, on the condition that I come back home to be the Principal of St. Barnabas Westwood, an Anglican Seminary in the making under Canon Peter Wagner who was running it only part-time. (The seminary ran out of funds while I was studying at the Graduate Theological Union, so I wasn't able to lead it.) I was touched by his ability to forget our differences. Despite his inability, as a white priest, to give up his racist views, insofar as the church and its leadership was concerned Bishop Burroughs encouraged African clergy. That was a break from his predecessors who had shown no inclination to develop African clergy. He was well informed about The Church Divinity School of The Pacific at the GTU. So that was one hurdle down.

The second hurdle was Rut. As a ZANU liberation activist, she had long ago set her mind to go and live in a free Zimbabwe. For more than six years, she was very much involved in raising funds and collecting clothes and medicine for our freedom fighters in Mozambique. On my part, I had been chairperson of the ZANU Branch in Europe excluding the U.K., and, in that regard, I shared the same dream to go to a newly liberated Zimbabwe as soon as possible. To go to the United States was not in Rut's scheme of things.

I was afraid of an absolute "no," from Ruth—so afraid, that instead of telling her right away, I spent a week in prayer, trying to figure out what to do. I couldn't overcome my fear of facing her directly, so after that week, I deliberately left Professor Garrett's letter open on the desk in our study, hoping Ruth would see it. Which she did.

After Rut read the letter, she put it in front of me, and said, "So, what are you going to do about it?"

I remember my mother and the children playing games in the living room as Rut and I sat down to make this big decision together. I told her that I had always had the desire to teach theology in Zimbabwe and an advanced degree at the Master's level would make it possible for me to get such a position. I said to her Zimbabwe will still be there in three years and we didn't have to rush home.

Rut was an amazing and sensitive person, and she could see how deeply sad I would be if I did not accept the scholarship. She had the capacity to see the long-term benefits of going to America. But my acceptance or rejection of the scholarship was now in her hands. So, it was a tremendous relief when she said, "Sebastian, if that is what you want, let's do it." I was filled with joy and I also heard again, the echoes of her Biblical namesake: "Wherever you go, I will go."

The third hurdle to overcome was my mother. Even after eighteen years of separation, I knew how she could be when something displeased her. And, indeed, when I told her, she was entirely against it. She gave me a long lecture about how I had been away from home for so long.

Then, she said a very chilling thing: "Zimbabwe is now free and so you are not coming home soon. All right – you go and when you finally decide to come to Zimbabwe, I will be dead." (*Zvakanaka endai munozondiona ndafa.*)

Trying to console her, I said we would come as soon as we finished our studies. She just looked at me and said no more.

Tragically, my mother's prediction turned out to be true.

* * *

A call to serve God's people has both advantages and disadvantages. Although Rut and I had made up our minds to leave Schalke, the leaving all the people we had come to care for was very hard. Our congregation in Gelsenkirchen-Schalke couldn't believe we were preparing to leave as we had been so happy working together to re-evangelize our parish. On the day we left, our parishioners were in mourning. It made us wonder whether we had made the right decision.

During the last week in the parish, I went around, as usual, doing my normal pastoral visits, when I was waylaid by the German national broadcasting station, Westdeutscher Rundfunk (WDR). The crew came to make a documentary film about my ministry under the title, "An African Missionary to Germany." The film was to be broadcast nationally to show that Germany had become a nation that needed missionaries from Africa. It aired on WDR as well as regional television stations and even won a prize.

There was an irony in the fact that the title of the documentary, "An African Missionary to Germany," which didn't sit well with some in church leadership. Many held stereotypical views of Africa and were of the view that Africa still needed missionaries from the West. What they didn't see was that many of their big church buildings that were once filled on Sundays had now become like museums. The larger German population was and still is no longer interested in going to church. Whether they liked it or not Germany was ripe for re-evangelization.

The following Sunday after the film crew was finished—our last in the parish—the church was so full not everyone could be seated. Sadly, Nyasha and Tinao kicked up a fuss in front of the large crowd as they had made it clear that they didn't want to leave. They behaved like children being handed over to foster parents they did not know. For them, life without Rut's parents—their beloved Oma and Opa—was too ghastly to contemplate.

Unbeknown to us, a group of parishioners had secretly left for Schiphol International Airport in the Netherlands together with the WDR-TV crew to see us off. My sister-in-law Elisabeth drove us to Schiphol with two miserable and tearful faces in the car as our children struggled to come to terms with this horrible separation from their grandparents. On arrival at the airport, we were surprised to be welcomed by the same people we thought we had left behind in Gelsenkirchen. Of course, our children continued to display their sad faces in front of the TV crew that was filming away.

CHAPTER TEN

Life in California

Seventeen hours after we left Amsterdam, we arrived at Los Angeles airport. The girls were sleepy and quiet through immigration. But once we arrived in Berkeley at the Church Divinity School of the Pacific more tears flowed. The temporary flat that had been arranged for us, while a bigger apartment was being painted, was a sad contrast to our spacious rooms in the Gelsenkirchen rectory.

But children are children. After a few hours of rest, we went out and found a nearby ice cream parlor, where we bought each child a scoop. American scoops are much larger than children are accustomed to in Germany. "Is this all mine?" Tinao exclaimed. Homesickness is a real thing, but ice cream scoops are, at least, a partial remedy.

* * *

We soon discovered that the Bay Area was a lot more attractive than Gelsenkirchen, and we quickly fell in love with our new home. Fisherman's Wharf, a snake park in Tilden, Livermore Observatory, were all lovely places to go with children. Near the campus was a rose garden with a well-equipped playground and a tennis court. The Berkeley community is an open one, and made us feel welcome almost immediately. Rut and I had been to several cities in Europe but never encountered such friendly people within as short a time period as we met in California; indeed, it favorably changed Rut's preconceptions about America.

Nyasha and Tinao quickly settled into their elementary school, which was just a bit uphill from our apartment. It did take them a bit of time to learn English—on the first day Tinao came home and cried for her beloved Oma in Germany. But there were many non-English speaking children from other parts of the world, and the school had enough assistant ESL teachers to help the children. And many thanks to Sesame Street which helped the children master their new language! After only three months they were speaking fluent English. How I wished I had had the same ability to learn German so fast; I had really struggled! Hillside School had incredible teachers who even bought books for the children using their own money. Many years after we had made Zimbabwe our permanent home, Rut and I often spoke fondly of Berkeley and San Francisco.

* * *

We had one major hiccup when we arrived in Berkeley. It took the Mercer Foundation more than two weeks to send our first grant money, and the small amount of money we brought ran out. Here we were, young people, with two children, in a still-strange city, without a penny to our name. It seems strange now, but even surrounded by friendly classmates and faculty, we had no idea what to do. We sat in our living room, with the girls playing happily in their small bedroom, not knowing their parents didn't have the wherewithal to buy them bread for the next morning's breakfast. At that moment I felt guilty for uprooting Rut and our children from their comfortable home in Germany, where we had everything. I felt ashamed and could only stare at the secondhand furniture, ashamed of the predicament I felt I had put us all in.

For many people of faith, there is a Bible verse they often turn to in times of want. "Therefore, I tell you, do not worry about your life, what you will eat or drink; about your body; what you will wear. Isn't life more than food, and the body more than clothes? Look at the birds of the air; they do not sow or reap or store in barns, and yet your heavenly Father feeds them. Are you not much more valuable than they" (Matthew 6:26)? But though we were very familiar with the verse, that night Rut and I were still exhausted from our travels, and terribly worried about our children, and the verse didn't come to mind.

Later that evening, there was a knock. It was Bishop Charles Shannon Mallory, the former Bishop of Botswana, who was now the first Bishop of El Camino Real, a diocese that had recently been formed in California. He was someone I hadn't met before, though I knew of him. He introduced himself and said that his parish, St. Mary's by the Sea in Pacific Grove, had sent him bearing welcoming gifts. Here, indeed, was an angel of the Lord, like the one who brought food to Elijah who had not taken any food with him, and after a long day's walk, lay down to sleep, wishing he was dead. "All at once an angel touched him and said, 'Get up and eat.' He looked around and, and there by his head was some bread" (Kings 19:5-8). God who knows our needs provides. In Matthew's gospel, Jesus says, "Therefore I tell you, do not worry about your life, what you will eat or drink; or about what your body, what you will wear" (Matthew 6:25).

It turned out that our friend Ruth Harris, the former missionary in Zambia, had returned and organized St. Mary's to donate money, food, and things that we might need to help start us off in our new country.

We were overcome by the generosity of St. Mary's and the bishop who had graciously agreed to act as an Angel of Hope. And it also confirmed our belief in God's providence.

* * *

In February 1982, eighteen months after our arrival, when I was in the middle of finalizing my dissertation, my mother passed from this life to the next. We didn't even know that she was in ill health, but it turned out that she had advanced esophageal cancer and died only a few hours after being admitted to Rusape Hospital. When I got the sad news, I remembered how she told me that if we went to America, she would die before we returned to Zimbabwe.

Nyasha and Tinao, who had become so attached to her, were grief-stricken and said they didn't want to go to Zimbabwe because their *mbuya* (grandmother) was no more. The seminary raised money in hopes that I would be able to fly home for her funeral, but because rural people in Zimbabwe hold funerals a day or two after a person dies, it would have been impossible for me to get there in time. I gratefully sent the money that was raised to help pay for funeral expenses.

CDSP held a requiem mass and Professor Garrett preached a profound sermon as if he had met and known my mother. I was, again, struck by what a saintly person he was.

After my ordination, my father said, "Now we have a priest in the family to bury us." I still couldn't travel to Rhodesia when he died in 1976 and, now again, I couldn't make it to my mother's funeral.

We did have Rut's mother join us for a few weeks, which the children enjoyed greatly.

* * *

St. Mary's-by-the-Sea is more than a two-hour drive from Berkeley. It was Ruth Harris' home parish and it also became our spiritual home. We often went down on weekends, so the children could watch the whales. Ruth Harris was a wonderful host and we were always welcome at her home.

The rector of St. Mary's, Father Dwight Edwards, was a graduate of CDSP and had studied Church History under Sam Garrett. He was delighted to know that Professor Garrett was also my Church History professor; with that connection we became friends. Decades later, when I was elected Bishop of Manicaland, Dwight sent me all the robes I needed as bishop. He called to congratulate me on my election, saying, "We would have loved for you and Rut to take a parish in this area but now we can see that God had other plans for you in your country. We will continue to hold you in our prayers." May his soul rest in peace and the hands of the blessed Almighty God.

* * *

The Berkeley community was and is a liberal community where people of different orientations feel at home. Gay and lesbian students in one of my classes helped me to understand who they are and the kind of discrimination they faced. I didn't have strong views about gay people, though I certainly had a lot of the stereotypical perceptions that I picked up from others. I shall always be grateful to the gay community for liberating me from those stereotypes. They were fantastic classmates and colleagues; friendly, kind, helpful, and above all committed to serving the church of God as priests.

It was a privilege when I was invited to an engagement party by two young classmates, Jerry and Gary. It was indeed a party with a difference because I had never seen one like it before. Had it been in Zimbabwe, we would have been condemned, if not arrested! Even as I write my memoir, innocent people are being butchered in Harare while taking part in peaceful demonstrations.

Under Mugabe's regime, gay people were kidnapped, disappeared and tortured by his henchmen. Mugabe compared gays and lesbians to dogs not worth living among "normal people." It makes one wonder about this use of the word "normal." Here Mugabe considered himself a worthier person to live than those he condemns as unfit human beings. In the United States, Donald Trump, another so-called "normal" human being, separated hundreds of refugee children from their parents. Such is the irony in our world, that such a person is considered normal and welcome in our society without suffering ridicule or prejudice. Normal people should be measured by the way they treat their fellow beings.

* * *

Rut and I were studying for graduate degrees at two different institutions— she at the University of California at Berkeley and I at the GTU. Luckily, that meant we could attend each other's graduation ceremonies, before our return to Germany via New York. Once we were back in Germany, we had only three weeks to pack and ship our household effects to Zimbabwe.

The return to Zimbabwe was not without some emotional trauma. My childhood memories of the harsh discrimination laws haunted me and I was very suspicious of every white "Rhodie" I met. Intellectually, I knew it was unfair of me, because some whites who remained after independence also felt liberated. But it takes a long time for childhood trauma to fade—if it ever does.

CHAPTER ELEVEN

Homecoming to Zimbabwe

Our coming to Zimbabwe in 1982 after so many years in the Diaspora was a joyful occasion but also sad because my parents were no more; I wished they could have been alive to be with us after we spent so many years abroad. But the joy of being home in a liberated Zimbabwe was overwhelming.

The flip side of coming home was that I did not have a job. I had been promised a job at the University of Zimbabwe, but it did not materialize. Faced with no prospects to support my young family, I even thought of going back to Germany to resume work at my former parish where the rector post was still vacant.

But when I expressed a desire to go back to Germany, Rut's response essentially was: "Over my dead body!" During those years of my exile, I had become an active supporter of ZANU, and Rut joined me in my determination to do everything I could, even if I couldn't physically return, to bring about the liberation of my country. I was elected chairman of the branch on the continent (which excluded Britain), and served in that post until I went to study in the United States.

And now, here we were in the former Rhodesia, now Zimbabwe, able to walk on the liberated soil of my birth. It is hard to convey to people who have not gone through this kind of struggle for independence the utter joy of such a moment. Everything was new to my wife and our children, and even for me to a large extent. I noticed even small things, like Africans who were once not allowed in certain places, or were humiliated constantly, now moving about freely and going with confidence about their business.

Yet I still had ambivalent feelings as I became accustomed to this new world. When I heard a white Rhodesian accent, I was reminded of the white police officer who invaded our village, forcibly evicted my family and neighbors, and was the cause of me losing my much-beloved model Benz.

Meanwhile, ZANU offered me a position as deputy director of cooperatives under Hon. M. Nyagumbo, which I turned down. A good number of comrades who had known me as an activist and chairman of the ZANU branch in Germany were surprised that I didn't take the position. But I told them I was trained to serve in the Church, not the state.

Bishop Peter Hatendi had been encouraging us to come home, and now that it turned out that the University of Zimbabwe didn't have the budget for the chaplaincy position he thought would be available, he was frantically trying to find a job for me. He found a part-time chaplain position for the Anglican UZ students, and he also appointed me co-rector of All Souls in Mount Pleasant. Meanwhile I secured a part-time lectureship in the UZ's Religious Studies Department. I now had three part-time jobs, which was a tough way to divide one's time, along with caring for young children. I remained hopeful that there would be one position where I could serve God's people.

* * *

While I was at a theological conference in Limuru, Kenya, Rut called to say that she thought she had found us a house in Mount Pleasant that she had no doubt I would like. The house on 8 Tunsgate, had everything that we could ever want: a beautiful and cultured garden with a glittering swimming pool, as well as a self-contained flat for our guests. We all liked it.

A year later, on November, 3 1983, Rufaro was born in the Mbuya Nehanda Maternity Ward. Opa and Oma arrived for her baptism.

Generally, Rufaro was a happy, satisfied child. But I remember one time, as a toddler, when she jumped into the swimming pool, giving her mother quite a shock. Luckily, she was not in the deep part, and Rut was close by, and a potentially deadly accident was averted. And when Rufaro learned how to swim, she became good at it and was thinking of becoming a professional swimmer—something her more academically minded parents discouraged. All three girls did very well at Arundel School and made us proud parents.

One time, Rufaro and a number of her friends formed swimming teams and were having a friendly race in our pool. Rufaro's best friend was on her team, but as they raced, her friend struggled. Rufaro went back to help her friend, and they lost, but for our youngest, helping a friend was more important than winning.

* * *

When Rut's parents, known as Opa (which meant grandfather) and Oma (grandmother) to our children, came to Zimbabwe for Rufaro's baptism, it was the first time they had visited Africa. Of course, they were educated people, and didn't have the kind of stereotypes that I often heard from my parishioners in Germany—like that Africa was a continent where the inhabitants lived side by side with wild animals and snakes; backward, undeveloped, poor, and victims of curable diseases. My in-laws were not coming to a dark Africa to see for themselves how their daughter was surviving in such a primitive setting. Rather they came with excitement to see the country they had heard a lot about from me and Rut.

Upon their arrival, Rut and I could barely come near to embrace them as Nyasha and Tinao were all over them. We would have liked to take them to places of interest, like Nyanga, Vumba, Chimanimani, Masvingo, or Victoria Falls, but they were too far away to comfortably drive to, especially for people in their seventies. However, Opa was very keen to go to St. Faith's Mission outside Rusape, my native district, because it was one of the oldest mission stations in Zimbabwe. I showed him the bell that had been hanging high on a tree for several generations. The sound of that bell was loud and could be heard a few miles away from the mission station. Opa, who was a very playful man even at 76-years old, climbed on a ladder that was attached to the tree and, to our amusement, started ringing the bell.

We took them to the church and discovered that the baptismal font, which was used when I was baptized as an infant, was still in use. During their visit, we met up with Bishop Hatendi, who as a boy used to be the bell ringer at St. Faith, and he and Opa enjoyed talking about it. This was the only time Opa came to Zimbabwe. I saw him in hospital in Gelsenkirchen when he was ill in 1986; a month later he died. Opa was a caring husband, a good father, and a wonderful pastor with a tremendous sense of humor. As for theology, he recognized Karl Barth as his teacher and no other. All theological discussions for him were about Karl Barth; as far as he was concerned, besides Karl Barth there was no theology worth talking about. At this time, there was a resurgence of theologies such as African Theology, Liberation theology from Latin America, Black American Liberation theology, Asian Theology. But in his opinion, all these theologies did not offer anything new that Karl Barth did not know and write about in his monumental volumes.

One thing I always appreciated about my father-in-law was that he was politically liberal and open-minded. He was against European oppression in Africa and Latin America. He listened to what we knew about the liberation struggle.

Opa and Oma enjoyed our home, especially our beautiful garden with trees and swimming pools. My father-in-law even spoiled our Doberman, Francis, by giving him biscuits through the window. After Opa passed on, Oma came and visited us in December 1986 and celebrated Christmas with us.

Five years later, in 1991, Oma was not well, and missed her grandchildren so much that she thought that she would be better off coming to Zimbabwe and being near us, rather than being alone in her flat in Gelsenkirchen. Rut's sister Elisabeth lived nearby in Gelsenkirchen, but being a school teacher, was away all day and Oma was left alone for hours. Whereas in Mount Pleasant, we had a maid in the house all the time, available whenever she needed help. She traveled to Zimbabwe accompanied by Elisabeth. She looked unwell but not in an alarming way. We put her in her favorite bedroom where she could watch the birds through the window making their nests in the big avocado tree outside. She was so happy and so were we. She did not mind having her grandchildren play around her bed as soon as they came from school. She loved it and we were so happy for her.

Her illness did not improve but somehow, she had the capacity to hide how unwell she was, indeed, it turned out these would be her last days on earth. On the day of her passing, I had just arrived from the university and as usual, I went to check on her to find out how she was doing. When I got in the room, she asked me to help her sit up in bed. I tried to help but she was too weak. She just managed to ask for *Abendmahl* (Holy Communion) and before I could do as she asked, with her still in my arms, she was gone! Gone! I was sad that I couldn't administer to her the Lord's Supper as she had wished. Yet, I was also tremendously touched by her faith that she desired this sacrament at the moment she intuitively felt that her time to leave this world was approaching.

I called Rut and Elisabeth from the kitchen and told them that she was gone.

My mother-in-law's final departure in my arms was an honor I shall always cherish. I loved Oma. During my time in Germany, Oma and Opa were my parents, as it were, and I was their son. When we got married, they helped us to settle down as a young couple. When our financial resources were limited, they were always there to help us. The prevailing political situation in Rhodesia prevented me from being with my parents when I became an adult, but God provided me with Oma and Opa in place of my parents. Both of them lived their faith and practiced it.

May they and their daughter, Rut, now in perpetual Glory, rest in peace.

CHAPTER TWELVE

Zimbabwe Council of Churches

I want to focus on one of the three jobs I took to support my young family because it's illustrative of how things stood in my newly independent country. I was appointed as a temporary co-rector of All Souls, a parish shared by two denominations, Anglican and Methodist. My co-rector was Methodist, and we altered Sundays. It was truly ecumenical; the only parish of its kind in Zimbabwe.

Though the ecumenical part worked well, the congregation was predominantly white, and mostly members of the Rhodesian Front—Ian Smith's party. The black members of the congregation were mostly ZANU-PF, including myself. Even my Methodist colleague was a member of the white Rhodesian Front and often castigated the new government, which irked me to my core.

On one particular Sunday, when it was my turn, the Bible text from the Anglican lectionary was from the Gospel of Matthew, Chapter 23. The theme was hypocrisy; a criticism of the religious practices of the Pharisees. In my introductory remarks, I described a hypocrite as a person who pretends to be what he is not. In his time, Jesus observed Pharisees, the male religious leaders, frequenting the Temple or synagogues for prayers, making sure people saw them as they raised their hands in prayer. According to Jesus' account in Matthew, Pharisees were self-righteous people; they had no compassion for those who suffered from physical or mental ailments. They condemned Jesus for healing the sick, they questioned Jesus' authority to do his healing on the Sabbath because even works of compassion and mercy were ruled out on the Sabbath. "You hypocrites!" Jesus said to the religious practitioners of his day, even to those who tithed, those who fasted, those who were known to be so very religious, and walked around in the community with pious faces. Jesus did not spare them in his time.

So, in my time, I turned to the congregation and said, Today we have our own hypocrites, different from those of Jesus' time. I gave an example about my former parish in Germany where some children would ask their parents the question, "Where were you when Hitler killed the Jews?" Some parents would not want to hear about Hitler, others would say, "Oh! that mad man, we were against him." Of course, anybody who was against Hitler risked his or her life, there, naturally, very few were willing to do so. So, hypocrisy played a big role in the life of many Germans, who said, "We did not support Hitler and his party." Yet millions were murdered in the name of the German people.

I continued with my sermon saying, "Today I am in Zimbabwe, I ask the same question to white members in our community: 'Where were white Christians when Ian Smith's regime created havoc for fifteen years against blacks whom he butchered and murdered?' The short answer I get from them is the same: 'We did not support him.' In today's Gospel, Jesus uses the word hypocrisy. He condemns religious hypocrisy of his day, practiced by religious authorities and the Pharisees."

My sermon did not go down well with two of the supporters of the now-defunct white regime of Ian Smith. They walked out in protest and temporarily left the parish. Sadly, they were both Anglicans who served on the parish council. They sought refuge in the next parish where they only stayed for a short time before they came back to All Souls after they had taken time to reflect deeply about what I had said in my sermon about the Pharisees and their religious lifestyle. They came back home because All Souls was their spiritual home and they were warmly welcomed back in the congregation. I don't know whether their coming back was a sign of repentance, but I do not doubt that they came back as changed persons.

At this time, there were still only a few black faces in the congregation and not a single one was on the council. The blacks had not yet fully recovered from what they had undergone during the colonial era and were taking time to assert themselves. When I left the congregation towards the end of 1984, the congregation was completely multi-racial.

Sometime after that sermon, as I was trying to deal with three part-time jobs and raising three young children, I was offered a job by the Zimbabwe Council of Churches as Urban and Rural Mission Secretary, a job that was previously held by Rev. Canaan Banana, before Independence. (Rev. Banana was Zimbabwe's first head of state, succeeded by Robert Mugabe after the elections.) He did a tremendous amount of work in creating an ecumenical minister's fraternity in the country that became a vanguard of political awareness among the pastors in the country. After Mugabe took over the presidency in 1987, Reverend Banana held a part-time lectureship in the Religious Department of the University of Zimbabwe, and he chose to spend some of his spare time in my chaplain's office. We became friends.

It is said that political enemies may have masterminded the accusations leveled against Reverend Banana that resulted in him being removed as titular head of state. He was not honored with the status of national hero he deserved as someone who was an early activist in the liberation struggle. I knew him as a friend before that, and someone who was called to serve God's people in this country.

I found the role of Urban and Rural Mission Secretary to be very exciting. I had a new sense of what it was to serve God's people in that ecumenical venture, "Your people are calling!" My job description was to encourage pastors to reactivate the ministers' fraternity. Practically speaking, that meant that I would get to know every corner of the country where a church was located.

I was able to visit poor and rich congregations in both rural and urban churches of all twenty-one denominations. Some mission centers were well developed while others were in poor condition. It was fascinating to see the way each denomination was programmed to do mission and evangelism. My focus was to encourage ministers to come up with projects in their congregations or mission stations that aimed at fighting the kind of poverty that ravaged many families, especially widows who were often left without recourse.

One thing I noted was that ZANU-PF had been giving handouts in some districts, which began a vicious cycle of dependency. Farmers who had been self-sustaining before, now relied on government largesse, which led to farmland being underutilized. I organized a few workshops on "Sustainable Development," to try to combat this trend.

About two years after our return to Zimbabwe, the position of ecumenical chaplain to the University of Zimbabwe was finally established. It was the job I had hoped for when I first came home, but it took that long to fund the post.

The job was very competitive, but I made it to the point where I was invited for an interview. I noticed that while other applicants' interviews took only about ten minutes, mine went on for an hour. I returned to my office dejected, feeling as though I had lost the job of my dreams.

A telephone call came through and, though I was not in the mood to talk, I picked up the phone. A voice said, "*Mzee* (brother), you got the job." I said, "This is Dr. Bakare," thinking the person on the other end was mistaken, and he said, "Yes, I know. Listen my, friend, you got the job as university chaplain on condition that you also lecture in the Religious Department part-time."

I was speechless but then found enough of a voice to thank my friend. For some reason, I thought of the Russian Cosmonaut Alexei Leonov, the first man to walk in space. I felt I was likewise floating freely in orbit. I left my office before the usual time and went home in order to break the good news to Rut. I got the job I always wanted I shouted; she knew that it was the job as senior ecumenical chaplain at the university and she was just as excited as I was.

Life became easier for us now that I was working full-time. The girls even got a raise in their weekly pocket money.

Sebastian Bakare, at 17, with his father Eric, 47, in 1957, in Bulawayo, in what was then Rhodesia (now Zimbabwe).

Sebastian Bakare and Ruth Büchsel, after their engagement, in Bonn, Germany, 1968.

Sebastian Bakare's parents, Eric and Eunice in Wedza, Zimbabwe, photographed in 1969 by Ruth when she traveled alone to meet them because Sebastian was banned from returning to what was then Rhodesia.

At the 1969 engagement of Sebastian and Ruth in Gelsenkirchen, Germany. Left to right: Ruth's brother Hans-Hermann, her mother Magdalena, Sebastian, Ruth, Ruth's father Hans and Ruth's sister Elisabeth.

Sebastian and Ruth's church wedding day, August 28, 1971, in Gelsenkirchen, Germany. Left to right: Westphalia Praeses Hans Thimme, Ruth, Sebastian, Ruth's father Pastor Hans Büchsel, and the Rev. Canon Beaumont Stevenson of Oxford, England.

Sebastian Bakare in 1973 when he was teaching comparative religion in a high school in Versmold, Germany.

Sebastian holds Nyasha and Ruth holds Tinao in a family photograph taken in Germany around 1976.

The Rev. Sebastian Bakare, Senior Chaplain of the University of Zimbabwe, walks in a graduation procession in the mid-1980s. Left to right: Dr. Ngwabi Bhebhe, Rev. Sebastian Bakare, Dr. Rob Blair, Dr. Chris Chetsanga, Dr. Phineas Makhurane, Dr. Dzingai Mutumbuka, President Canaan Banana, Dr. Walter Kamba.

The Rev. Sebastian Bakare at the shrine of Bernard Mzeki in Marondera, Zimbabwe, during his consecration as Bishop of Manicaland in 1999.

Governor Kenneth Manyonda of Manicaland welcomes Bishop Bakare to the province upon the occasion of his enthronement in the Cathedral of St. John's in Mutare in 1999.

Ruth Bakare, on the day of the 1999 consecration of Sebastian as Bishop of Manicaland,
at Bernard Mzeki shrine, Marondera, Zimbabwe.

Sebastian Bakare, on the day of his consecration as Bishop of Manicaland in 1999, at
Bernard Mzeki shrine, in Marondera, Zimbabwe.

Sebastian and Ruth Bakare at St. Andrew's, Scotland, during a conference on mission and evangelism in the early 2000s.

Sebastian and Ruth Bakare with a birthday cake given by the Mother's Union in honor of Ruth's birthday in 2004, Mutare, Zimbabwe.

Bishop Sebastian Bakare receives the 2008 Swedish Per Anger Prize for his long-standing efforts working for democracy in Zimbabwe.

Bishop Sebastian Bakare preaches in 2008 in Stockholm, Sweden upon the occasion of being awarded the Per Anger Prize.

Bishop Sebastian Bakare and his wife Ruth being awarded honorary doctorates in 2010 from Church Divinity School of the Pacific, Berkeley, California.

Bishop Sebastian Bakare and his then 4-year-old granddaughter Nomsa Nganang in November 2013 at home in Mutare, Zimbabwe, on the day celebrating 50 years of his ordination as a priest.

The Bakare family at home in Mutare in 2014. Left to right: Nyasha, Rufaro, Sebastian, Ruth, Nomsa, and Tinao.

Bishop Sebastian Bakare, in Princeton, New Jersey in 2023.

CHAPTER THIRTEEN

Challenges of a University Chaplain

The University of Zimbabwe as an institution of higher learning was very different in its governance structures and ethos than the Anglican Church. The church's governing structure is based on Canon Law, while its ethos is based on the Book of Common Prayer, or the BCP as church members often shorten it. The BCP is used worldwide by members of the communion and also as an identity for its members.

Now here I was, invited to be a pastor of a cosmopolitan institution with more than eighty-one religious denominations, working for the university or attending as students, including various Christian denominations, and followers of traditional tribal religions, Islam, Baha'I, and Hindus. Luckily, I had the opportunity to take a comparative religions course at the Graduate Theological Union that was very helpful, especially when it came to pastoral counseling, which is a major component of the job of a university chaplain.

The Vice-Chancellor of the University welcomed me to the university community in a friendly and brief meeting, telling me he was happy to have a full-time pastor on campus. Then he said, "Dr. Bakare, since you are the first incumbent to hold the office of Senior Ecumenical Chaplain of this office institution, all that I ask you is to write your job description and give me a copy and send the other copy to the Registrar's Office."

It was an honor to write my job description and I did so happily. That job description gives an idea of how I approached my new position:

JOB DESCRIPTION FOR SENIOR CHAPLAIN

I described the university as a congregation, and my assignment was a cure of souls for the university's students and staff.

Specific duties included:
To plan and organize university services;
To take funeral and wedding services for staff members and students;
To visit the sick in hospital and liaise with local pastors if the patient was from their congregation;
To form a viable ecumenical community with honorary chaplains;
To liaise with city pastors in case of hospital visits be there a patient from their congregation;
To take a mediating role between members of the university of the UZ community and outsiders;
To be the chief spiritual shepherd of the university.

My job description would be put to the test in the real world as political developments in Zimbabwe did not leave the university untouched.

* * *

The University community comprised about 9,000, including faculty, administration, students, and staff. A large proportion of the students came from poor families in rural areas. The rural population had a lot of anger against government policies; coming together at university gave them the opportunity to share their common national concerns, which led to demonstrations. When political leadership forbids freedom of speech, the environment can often become very volatile. Demonstrators are often shot on sight, journalists are arrested, and people live in fear of their government.

When I came to the university, demonstrations were constant. Students and police regarded each other as enemies. Students had their grievances and the riot police had their obligation to keep law and order. My mission was to preach the gospel of peace, reconciliation, and healing. I organized a series of meetings with two antagonistic groups: the Student Representative Council and senior public relations police officers. The workshops were successful and the result was that in the end they recognized each other as brothers and sisters. There were no more demonstrations but the effects of tear gassings, beatings, and nights spent in police custody took time to be forgotten. Hence the need for healing.

From then on, I focused my ministry on peace, justice, and forgiveness. Fortunately, Christian students had established their own denominations' societies which met once per week in the evenings to discuss issues affecting their lives on campus, including the meaning of the word reconciliation.

Yet, sometimes, when I went home, I was in disbelief that our African government was resorting to mistreating students—or any group—using the same tear gas and dogs as did the colonial regime of Ian Smith.

Serving as Ecumenical Chaplain was one of the highest points of my call to holy orders. Daunting as my pastoral work might have appeared it offered me challenges and opportunities which made me feel fulfilled to serve my people.

* * *

In the fall of 1988, the Zimbabwe newspaper, *The Bulawayo Chronicle*, exposed the so-called Willowvale Scandal, where several ministers and senior civil servants were allowed to buy cars at a car plant in Willowvale, near Harare, at wholesale prices, but then sometimes sold them for a huge markup. The exposure of the scandal at the Willowvale car plant angered the public who were experiencing financial hardship and high unemployment. University students were angry because they viewed the corruption by the government officials as robbing them of a chance for their future.

Willowvale was only one symptom of the corruption that had already penetrated every sector in Zimbabwe. The elite had diamonds and gold smuggled out of the country for their enrichment. Those in high positions after independence were trying to lay their hands on all kinds of goods without paying for them. The judiciary and the police were also showing signs of professional and ethical decay as the culprits responsible for the corruption were not arrested; they considered themselves above the law.

This official corruption did not sit well with our university students, especially at a time when the government grants that they depended upon were not being released. After the Chronicle published its story, the leadership of the student council came to my office, seeking advice about what they could do. Though I said I wasn't in a position to tell them what to do, I said there were two alternatives. They could keep quiet and avoid being arrested. Or they could be public in their condemnation of the abuse of power and corruption.

At first, there was relative peace on campus. But one day a blind student, who is now a professor in Canada, let me know that a serious student demonstration was being organized and there would be no lectures the next day. Meanwhile, a few police officers were spotted and attacked by students. That action provoked the wrath of the riot police who ruthlessly descended on campus in numbers, tear-gassing, and beating everybody they came across. This time the reasons for the demonstrations were different than earlier; it was against the corruption of political leaders abusing their power. Running battles developed across campus—students armed with stones in their hands and the riot police with cans of tear gas.

One time the battle was pitched at the basketball grounds; it was as though David and Goliath were battling on a basketball court. I went to the basketball courts directly from the chapel and stood in the middle of the students and the police who were confronting each other. I was expecting one side to provoke the other, but perhaps my appearance—looking to the fighters, no doubt, like a lunatic—stopped them from what they were planning. I said, "Here we are, fathers, sons and daughters, sisters and brothers, cousins and nephews, and neighbors from various villages and cities in our free Zimbabwe. Why are we armed with stones and tear gas, ready to harm each other, brothers and sisters?"

The two groups were dead silent, and I had no idea what would happen next. Then, one by one, the students dropped the stones from their hands. The riot police, likewise, put their tear gas cans away. I invited all to come and shake my hand. The student ringleader came first to take my hand, and the rest followed. I did not even pray—I left everything in God's hands.

We walked together peacefully as one group towards the chapel, joking with each other like friends and no longer as enemies. The last bits of tear gas that had polluted the entire campus evaporated in the thin air. To this day I cannot remember what pushed me into that dangerous situation where I could have been badly hurt. I admit that I was probably stupid and naive but God protected us all from a potentially deadly situation. I informed the Vice-Chancellor that the students and police had agreed to a ceasefire, though I told him I did not know how long it was going to hold. And indeed, soon after, the students began demonstrating again because the government wasn't forthcoming in condemning corruption.

As campus demonstrations continued, Zimbabwe's Minister of Higher Education, Fay Chung, was sent to address the students, about 5,000 of whom filled the University's Great Hall. (I was seated in the back watching all that transpired.) But Chung was shouted down and not given a chance to speak. Next up was Vice President J. Nkomo, the Father of the Nation, who the government sent because they thought the students would respect him. But instead of addressing corruption, he began with a speech about the history of the liberation movement, and the benefits he said it brought to the people of Zimbabwe. A student, very small in stature, stood up and demanded, "Your excellency, we are not interested in the history of liberation, but what you are doing about corruption!" The entire hall erupted.

Nkomo banged the table in front of him and walked out. As he walked down the long aisle of the Great Hall, there were more cheers, jeers, and whistles. I was torn about what I had just seen. On the one hand, I had never seen such direct disrespectful behavior by young people toward their elders in my life and I felt very unhappy about my role as a pastor to students who behaved like hooligans. On the other hand, Nkomo made a blunder by not first asking the students about their grievances; he forgot that he was speaking to students with empty stomachs. After this incident, I kept on asking myself what the call to "serve God's people" truly meant. Each day brought different ways to be of service; some situations were fulfilling, but others were spiritually draining.

When Reverend Ffrancon-Jones said in his sermon, "Your people are calling," it was an invitation to us high school students to become aware of what it meant to serve our people, who at that time were under siege by an oppressive regime of white settles, where we as black people had no right to determine our future, including our right to vote. Now, Zimbabwe was ostensibly free, but at the same time, our students were not free to express themselves even under a black government. They faced arrests and were often tear gassed if they dared to demonstrate against the regime, not unlike African students under the colonial regime. The black government had become more oppressive and corrupt than its predecessor. Ironically, some political leaders now in government had gone through the same experience under the white regime. They were arrested, expelled, imprisoned for years, even tortured. Now it was their turn to do the same to their own kith and kin. I call this a vicious circle of madness that never seems to end.

I fully understood how the students felt. Here they didn't even have enough to eat, yet they watched the countries' political leadership taking national resources as their personal property. The campus was torn apart by running battles, with tear gas everywhere. It wasn't possible to move about without holding a wet towel to your face to be able to breathe, as the gas can be suffocating. It was a very ugly experience for the university community.

One morning as I was on my way to the city, the minister of education, Ignatius Chombo, drove up behind me and motioned that he wanted to talk to me, so I pulled over to the side of the road. He pulled his black Mercedes Benz over He pulled up next to my small "people's car"—a VW Golf—in his black Mercedes Benz. He said, "Dr. Bakare, you are not preaching hard enough to the students. Look at what they are doing." I told him, "The students are starving and you guys are eating to the full. You haven't paid students their grants for a month now—where do you think they get their food from?" The good minister barely replied and drove off at a high speed. I was happy I delivered my message. In serving people, one gets more criticism than praise. I was learning to accept whatever people had to say about my ministry.

Two students, the President of SRC, A. G O. Mutambara, and Enoch Chikweche (Gwisai) who was the SRC General Secretary, were arrested and taken to the city's central police station. There was a BBC report that they had been shot dead. In the early hours of the morning, the Vice-Chancellor called me asking me to go to the police station and find out if the report was true. When I showed up at the station, demanding to know the truth, a youthful-looking police officer gave me a horrified look. He went out and came back with his boss who told me that the two students were alive and I should come back that afternoon if I wanted to talk to them.

The arrests meant that there was going to be no reconciliation between the students and the police. I was able to deliver the good news that the arrested students were alive, and I had been invited back to speak to them. I arranged a meeting between police commissioners and SRC members in an attempt to defuse hostilities. It seemed to work, for a short time, but then another very serious and aggressive demonstration started in one of the students' residences. This time, a group of riot police came in full battle mode. Students were no match for the riot police.

After the police withdrew after that latest confrontation, the Vice-Chancellor and the Registrar summoned students to the Great Hall, told them that the university was closed and they should all go home.

That evening the university was empty. I missed the students so much. It was time for me to go home and, as usual, I went to lock up the chapel. I went into the sacristy and discovered a student who had hidden out in the chapel, cowering in a corner. At first, when he heard me, he thought I was the police coming to find him and give him a beating. He was incredibly happy to see it was me.

Within a week, the students were called back to university and they finally started receiving their grants.

After the demonstrations, I started a lecture series: *Peace and Justice, the Role of the State and Citizens*, delivered by both faculty and students, followed by discussions. The series was very popular with students and lecturers alike, who found it helpful to be able to share testimonies about their faith.

* * *

When the University was reopened after a week, bishops and the clergy in greater Harare remained silent. Not a single pastor or bishop called to find out how I was managing or surviving that war-like situation. I lost my confidence in the "Good Shepherds" of my nation.

When our five-year-old daughter saw all that was happening on campus, she declared that she would like to skip university when she grew up, that's how bad the situation was. Now that I am retired, and I'm reviewing my 60-year ministry, I realize that my chaplaincy at the university was one of the most trying times I experienced. Rut was very much concerned about my security and I was indeed risking my life, though she never asked me not to go and seek peace between two warring groups. The situation was ugly and it made human beings behave in a very strange way; almost to the point of acting insane. But a call to serve God's people is a call to carry the cross, a call to discipleship, and a call to self-denial. I thank God to have had this opportunity and it was by His grace that I was allowed to serve my people in this way. God was there with me and they helped me escape attack by the riot police.

* * *

After the student leaders were released, the SRC announced what they called a celebration meeting in the Great Hall. It was my general practice to be present at their meetings so I could hear the students' concerns, and I was seated in the back as was my custom. Before the beginning of the ceremony, Arthur Mutambara, who was serving as master of ceremonies, called out, "Senior Chaplain, if you are present, please come to the podium." I expected to be asked to say an opening prayer, as had often been requested before.

On the podium in front of me was a large closed cardboard box about a meter high. Mutambara, along with Enock Chikweche, opened the box to reveal a copper crucifix. He lifted it high, showing it to the packed Great Hall. Then, he handed the cross to me, saying, "Senior Chaplain, on behalf of the student body, I give you this cross as a symbol of a good pastor who cares for his flock in this university community." I was emotionally overcome by this gesture from the students.

Mutambara then spoke about the tear gas, the beatings, and the injuries sustained by students. He said I was with them during those battles and that I had made the University Chapel a sanctuary for those who weren't able to escape the suffocating clouds of tear gas. "The Senior Chaplain never abandoned us at a time when other members of the staff were nowhere to be seen around the university," he said.

I felt humbled by the students' gestures. In response to the students for the priceless gift of a crucifix, I thanked them, referring to their gift and celebration as my "mini-ordination." The Crucifix hangs today in my chapel as a precious gift from my flock at the University of Zimbabwe. My chaplaincy at the university allowed me to minister to the vibrant younger generation and share in their hopes and fears. Yet, the first struggles toward a free and just society were not promising to be easy ones.

Then, and now, I take instruction from that call in Isaiah, Chapter 6: "Your people are calling." When Isaiah accepted God's call to be an ambassador of peace, it was in a political and volatile region with Nebuchadnezzar poised to invade the small Kingdom of Judah. And it's not as though Judah was populated by holy people—far from it. As the prophet says: "'Woe is me!' I cried. 'I am ruined! For I am a man of unclean lips, and I live among people of unclean lips and my eyes have seen the King, the Lord Almighty'" (Isaiah 6:5).

I didn't understand why Isaiah, Chapter 6 was read at my three ordination services: deacon, priest, and bishop. Little did I know that one day in my vocation as a priest, I would be facing perpetrators of a dictatorial system that denied the majority freedom of speech; a political system whose leaders thrived on corruption. Now, as a retired bishop, among my regrets, are that I did not do enough of what I ought to have done, as Zimbabwe's leadership continues to pursue a route that is leading to disaster for my country.

* * *

During this time, we had the joy of a visit from our dear friends, Herman and Mary Waetjen. Herman Waetjen was taking a sabbatical year and had accepted our invitation to come and teach the New Testament in the University of Zimbabwe's religion department.

During Christmas break our two families traveled to Lake Kariba, which was formed by a huge dam. The lake is famous for its hippopotamus and tiger fish. One day, we went out fishing and I had the bad luck to catch a big tiger fish that fought me. I was having trouble landing it and called out Herman to help as he is an experienced fisherman. But no—my good friend said it was my fish, so I had to reel it in! Which I eventually did after being dragged from one end of the boat to the other. The fish was so big that Rufaro, who was then two-and-a-half, was too scared to look at it. The huge fish easily fed the seven of us for dinner. The one problem was that our trip to Kariba was unbearably hot, which was hard for our friends, accustomed to the moderate climate of northern California. (Conversely, in July when we visited Nyanga, a tourist location because of its natural beauty—nearby is Mount Nyangani, the highest mountain in Zimbabwe—it was bitterly cold.)

Many years after they visited, the Waetjens still remembered our trip and would often write to us, or talk about it when we were able to phone. Herman and Mary were always a source of comfort and inspiration to us.

CHAPTER FOURTEEN

A Call to Serve Manicaland

The Diocese of Manicaland was formed in 1981 and Bishop Elijah Masuku was their first bishop. So, when I was elected Bishop in 1999, I was only the diocese's second bishop. The diocese covers the Province of Manicaland with the greatest number of churchgoers in Zimbabwe.

This call to serve the church as a Bishop came as a surprise to me. The Bishop is called first to be the chief shepherd of the flock of God. I already had served as a deacon, priest, archdeacon, canon of the Cathedral, ordination candidates' chaplain, secretary for the urban and rural mission, lecturer in the Religious Department of the University, and finally as senior ecumenical chaplain. But a call to be Bishop—the chief shepherd of the flock of God—that I felt was different altogether, and too big a call for me. Initially, I said no. Besides not being interested in the role, I was happy with what I was doing.

Yet, I couldn't shake my original inspiration for the ordained ministry—Isaiah's response to God: Here am I. Send me. Perhaps this was a naive response, where I didn't fully count the cost of such an undertaking. So, after much thought, I reluctantly agreed to come to Manicaland to serve as their Bishop. I assured myself that God had plans for what he wanted me to be. I didn't want to be like Jonah who refused but found himself on the shores of Nineveh on God's mission.

So, when I was delivering my first sermon in the Cathedral of St. John's the Baptist, I turned, once again to Isaiah's words, "Here am I. Send me." I told the congregation that those words from Isaiah's unclean lips had been a burden to me since my seminary days. But I still hadn't forgotten that those words, from the lips of my school principal, also a priest, were preached during the very week that Ghana was celebrating its independence from British colonial rule. And that he had put the text in the context of Rhodesia, saying to us students, God is calling you to liberate your people from British rule so that you can be like Ghana.

Manicaland is a province where the people live in poverty, though the land itself is endowed with a multitude of natural resources. Consequently, the congregations were not materially well off, though they were spiritually rich. And so, in my first sermon, I raised this question, What is my mission to this diocese, to the congregations, to men and women in rural and urban centers? And then, the even bigger question: What is our mission? The good news that I bring is to share God's word that liberates us from the burdens that we carry day by day. There is poverty, hunger, disease, corruption, selfishness, oppression, denial of human rights, regionalism, and inequality. We have to pray for God's grace to preach the gospel that liberates us.

Then I continued: The Church of God is on a mission to liberate us from the scourge of abject poverty, and the scourge of those things which make life so difficult to bear—and among them, corruption, selfishness, oppression, denial of human rights, inequality—those are sins that are caused by greedy leadership. Jesus commissioned his disciples to continue with his mission to all nations and we are to follow the footprints of his disciples and participate in God's Mission. Each one of us has a missionary responsibility against corruption, poverty, oppression and violence in our society. A diocese that is not involved in condemning such ills in society, is in denial of its mission.

May I once more appeal and remind ourselves that, as members of the Anglican Diocese of Manicaland and Zimbabwe, we are called to do God's Mission, and doing God's mission means accepting his call to fight enemies with activities that promote love, peace, and justice in our communities. As a diocese, responding to such a call demands self–denial. As your bishop, I am inviting you to do the little you can and God himself will do the rest. Unless each one of us says—I am here. Send me.—We cannot earnestly pray your Kingdom comes on earth as it is in heaven.

Then, there was the issue of leaving my beloved students to accept the call as Bishop, as well as the impact on my family. The day I was elected, I received a phone call while I was chairing a worship committee meeting with students in my office. The call was from Archbishop K. W. Makhulu, telling me that I had been elected Bishop of Manicaland. Some students must have noticed that my face had dropped and my voice changed. I did not tell them what the phone call was about. My concern was about my wife, what to say to her and Rufaro when I got home. (And, indeed, when I broke the news, Rufaro was full of anxious questions about her school, her friends, her mother's job—and I didn't have a good answer for her.) My other two daughters were overseas in school, so I had time to break the news to them that this new call would mean moving away from Mount Pleasant—the place they called their home—to Mutare.

But because Manicaland is so very poor, I could not turn away from the call to minister to the poorest of God's people.

The Diocese of Manicaland is densely populated. There are many congregations and several schools but few health centers. And it's a large area—it took me almost six months to familiarize myself with all the congregations and public institutions. And there were physical limitations to traveling to be with the people, as most of the rural roads were impassable during the rainy season. There are no bridges, so after a rainfall, one cannot cross over the flooded rivers.

But despite harsh rural conditions, Rut and I saw signs that church members were excited about our invitation to mission and evangelism training, indeed, the response was beyond our expectations. We started by focusing on a program of training trainers, so that they, in turn, could lead local study groups.

One thing I noticed in my travels was that the poor rural people seemed happier than the rich I met in the cities, who were always worried about their fortunes. As the Bible says, "The sleep of laborers is sweet, whether he eats little or much, but the abundance of a rich person permits him no sleep" (Ecclesiastes 5:12). By this observation, I am not glorifying the state of the poor because they have been denied access to a better living by those in power. But what I saw was that what was needed were sustainable projects so that those living in the country could produce agricultural products to reduce their dependence on government handouts, made mostly to buy their vote. Sustainable projects would instill self-respect and dignity for the rural poor.

After intensive teaching on stewardship, we started seeing church contributions increase. The so-called poor parishes were giving more support to the clergy than those that were considered rich. The poor congregations developed a sense of ownership of their church property faster than

I expected. We soon had enough money to pay stipends for the clergy. The idea of self-reliance was yielding tangible results.

As I said, the personal sacrifices in taking on this huge task were many, especially for my family. But my wife and I had come a long way together, taking many risks along the way. Sometimes, there were painful decisions to be made like when we left behind our dear ones in Germany; those were moments that tested our faith.

And having a far-flung family added to the stress of making decisions together as a cohesive family unit. I'll never forget before we moved to Mutare, how we decided to put our beloved family dog, Francis, to sleep because of old age and illness. Nyasha was in school abroad at the time, and when we told her, after the fact, she was furious with us for not including her in the decision. I felt terrible about it, but we couldn't watch a much-loved dog suffer anymore. Up to this day, our dog Francis is fondly remembered and spoken of with great love.

CHAPTER FIFTEEN

Service to the Church in Zimbabwe and Beyond

Throughout my time of active service to the church, I had the good fortune to serve on several international commissions. Each one had its own contribution to make, and each contributed to my broader understanding of what it meant to be called to a life of service. I hope, in some small way, I also contributed to the life of the church in the world through this service. There were a number of these commissions that I was blessed to have worked with—both national and international—I will touch on a few of them here.

Before I recount my service on international commissions, I want to note that at home, I was invited to serve the nation on various boards related to social development and education—too numerous to include in this narrative—the professional resume that I have included as an appendix lists many of them. But there is one unforgettable instance that is a good example of the stresses on a new nation. I was on the National Aids Council, when I and four other members, discovered that the minister of health was demanding that funds raised to combat HIV be redirected to pay the salaries of civil service employees in his ministry. We protested as we considered his suggestion immoral and unethical; at the time, we didn't know that corruption was widely spreading in all the government ministries. We were not surprised to receive a letter of dismissal.

But I also would be remiss if I only noted some of the problems of these local boards. Indeed, I got to know people who served on these boards who were experts in their fields and were ready to share their experiences with other board members. They served in an unassuming and generous manner; I was happy to know we had intellectuals and professionals who were willing to help build our new nation.

ANGLICAN STANDING COMMISSION ON MISSION AND EVANGELISM

In 1988, I was invited to join the Anglican standing commission on Mission and Evangelism. Being a member of this commission would be an honor; a way for me to serve my church at a truly global level. It would broaden my Anglican perspective and I would understand more about the church's work on mission and evangelism. To serve on any international commission meant to go beyond the boundaries of Zimbabwe. I shall always be grateful to those who considered me worthy to serve on this—and other international commissions.

The first meeting was in London and all twenty-two Anglican provinces were present.

We first met at St. Andrew's, Tavistock, for orientation to familiarize ourselves with the agenda of the commission. Participants consisted of men and women, ordained and laity. We even had one religious sister in attendance. Our task was to study and recommend to the Anglican Communion how the church was fulfilling its mandate on mission and evangelism at the contextual level. Among other things, we were asked to pay special attention to leadership training and ministerial formation for mission, justice, and peacebuilding. We identified a wide range of specific tasks related to these areas, including the ongoing tensions and difficulties for Christians worldwide living under the shadow of deadly diseases, terrorism, oppression, violence, and poverty. Personally, it was a challenging experience for me to join this commission with so many well-informed and competent participants. As a person from the developing continent of Africa, I was quite familiar with some of the issues faced by the church in the area covered by our mandate, though not in the depth that other commission members had studied them.

Our task was to go to different countries to see the context in which the church was carrying out its work. And a year after this organizing meeting in England, the very next venue that the commission wanted to come to was Harare. Of course, because that was my country, I was expected to host it, which gave me some pause. Fortunately, I had a year to prepare and

SERVICE TO THE CHURCH IN ZIMBABWE AND BEYOND

I had also, in the meanwhile, become Archdeacon of Harare West. To my relief, the visit went off without a hitch.

As we traveled from country to country, we became more and more aware of the fact that mission and evangelism is the real backbone of the church, and indeed, the very reason for the existence of the Anglican Communion. We became more convinced that the relevance of the Gospel would be obscured if the challenges and opportunities we encountered in different national contexts were not given the attention they deserved.

My brief recollections of countries the commission visited where I was in attendance follow. (The commission visited more countries, but I didn't always travel with them.)

Harare, Zimbabwe.

The Commission came to Zimbabwe when HIV was at its highest, claiming many lives. It was the most challenging period for the church in the country. Though a few drugs were available, only the rich could afford them, and they didn't cure the disease. (As a side note: I am so proud of my daughter Nyasha, who, as a physician, joined a team at Johnson and Johnson that helps to develop treatments aimed at preventing and curing diseases such as HIV, and other diseases like tuberculosis and leprosy that claim many lives, especially in Africa.) In Harare, the Commission heard sad and touching testimony from a young priest who was a rector of a very big parish. He told them that he spent most of his pastoral work at the cemeteries burying the dead, with an average of four-to-five funeral services per week in his parish. For him, the context of the church's mission and evangelism was preaching to the grieving members of the family and mourners.

Kempton Park, South Africa.

A year later, we visited Kempton Park, just outside of Johannesburg. One of the commissioner's brothers had passed away of HIV, and we were all invited to attend the funeral service. We went to Tembisa cemetery, which covers a huge area. When we got there, it took us some time to find the right gravesite because the whole area had so many groups of people burying their dead. We witnessed another context of the church doing mission and evangelism at a cemetery. It was an all-too-common feature in Africa at that time.

Kingston, Jamaica.

Kingston had just passed through a spate of violence before we arrived; I remember there were tensions and a general sense of insecurity. Nonetheless, we were housed in a nice hotel, aptly named the Runaway Bay Hotel. And the Jamaica assistant bishop, who was in our group, kept us abreast of the problems with drugs, unemployment, violence, and poverty from which the country suffered. That was the context in which mission and evangelism were playing out in Jamaica. We were so busy that we had little time for sightseeing, other than a brief tour of Kingston and Spanish Town, though we did visit the Bob Marley Museum, which was fascinating.

There was one nerve-wracking drama when I was on my way to Kingston through New York's John F. Kennedy airport. As I was waiting for my flight, three vicious dogs suddenly charged toward me, then stopped and began sniffing my bags. The white police officers must have assumed I was a drug baron on my way to Jamaica and so sent their dogs after my baggage. When the dogs found nothing, the officers just took off with their dogs without a word of apology. I certainly noticed that when I was traveling through Europe, nobody set dogs on me. I concluded that the whole vigilante exercise at JFK was racially motivated.

Recife, Brazil.

We were staying in a nice hotel by the beach, so what a shock it was for us to visit a church that was in the middle of a garbage dump where thousands of people lived in shelters that were mere plastic sheets. The smell from the dump in the church was unbearable. A young woman priest was in charge of the congregation and was doing fantastic mission and evangelism work among the homeless people of Recife. Her name was Semeia, which in Greek means seed. And she was indeed sowing seeds of mission and evangelism among the homeless poor in the community. We were impressed beyond measure with her commitment.

Paphos, Cyprus.

The commission met to put together our final report in Cyprus, about eight years after I first joined. It seemed like a meaningful place to reflect on mission and evangelism in the church as Cyprus has great meaning in the New

Testament. Paphos is where St. Paul first landed when he made his journey to Cyprus. The island is also the location of the Tomb of Lazarus, the same Lazarus who Jesus raised from the dead. Sometime after that miracle, Lazarus returned to his native land of Cyprus because of persecution in Jerusalem and then, according to legend, died there thirty years later. The tomb is in an area controlled by the Turkish government, and not by the Cypriots. Because of that, as we were told by an Anglican bishop, Christians weren't allowed to build churches in the region, but had to meet in so-called "church houses." That was the context in which the church was—and still is—doing its mission and evangelism work in the Middle East.

A lot more was happening in the Communion where the Anglican Church was being called upon to serve the people of God. A call to serve God is a risky one and yet it is in such situations where God gives his grace to those he invites to serve his people. Old Testament Prophets went through it; early church fathers and many martyrs have gone the same route. But they were not alone. The Lord Jesus said to his disciples, "And surely I am with you always, to the very end of the age" (Matthew 28:20). The mission and evangelism of the church begin and end with Jesus, who is the High Commissioner for all time.

As the commission members shared our stories in preparing our final report, I felt that the Anglican Communion was on the right track in its attempt to do mission and evangelism in various social and political contexts. Before I mostly had a perspective of Anglican mission and evangelism in the African context, but this gave me a broader understanding of other parts of the world. I will not forget the members I got to know during the eight years of working together on the commissions and the various places we visited during our annual meetings. They remain memorable and a part of my very being.

INTER-ANGLICAN COMMUNION AND THE LUTHERAN WORLD FEDERATION

In the1980s, Anglicans and Lutherans began formal conversations about a possible partnership at an international level. Both denominations are worldwide communions, formally called the Anglican Communion and the Lutheran World Federation. Regional dialogues were formed in Africa, Europe, Asia, and North and South America. I represented the Church Province of Central Africa and became co-chair with Dr. A. Moyo who represented the Lutherans in Africa. The first international meeting was held in the United States at Virginia Theological Seminary in 2000, followed by a meeting in Reykjavik, Iceland in 2001, and then the last, in Porto Alegre, Brazil in 2002. I remember vividly swimming in the lakes warmed by geysers while surrounded by snow in Reykjavik; what a contrast to my swimming in the temperate climate of Zimbabwe.

Our mandate was to discuss common shared practices found in both traditions such as sacraments of ordination, baptism, and Eucharist. The dialogue was intended to help the two denominations relate to each other by having this common understanding of the sacraments. The aim was to make members of the two denominations feel at home in each other's churches.

Among the reasons that it was felt that the two churches could form a partnership is that Anglicans and Lutherans have a lot in common in their traditions. The liturgy in the Anglican Book of Common Prayer and the Lutheran prayer book is similar. They also share a common understanding of the sacraments of baptism, the Eucharist, and the ordained ministry. What resulted from these discussions was that each church kept its own organizations, but they agreed to exchange pulpits. Indeed, I was in an exchange program when I took charge of a Lutheran parish in Germany, where I felt very much at home. At the University of Zimbabwe as senior ecumenical chaplain, I and Dr. A. Moyo had a common program for the students from the two denominations; the students appreciated sharing services from both denominations.

WORLD COUNCIL OF CHURCHES—FAITH AND ORDER COMMISSION

I attended the Faith and Order Commission in Santiago de Compostela, Spain held in 1993. It was the first time that the Russian Orthodox Church felt free to attend, as the Soviet Union had recently dissolved in 1991. I was fascinated to learn about orthodox ecclesiology, especially after they had been politically cut off from the rest of Christendom by the communist regime. However, we found that the Russian Orthodox theologians were very conservative and generally unwilling to listen to other theological points of view. We felt sorry for them—but I don't mean that in a patronizing sense—more the way one feels toward a brother or sister who is struggling.

Despite theological differences, it was so moving to worship together in the awesome Santiago de Compostela Cathedral with its unique bells. Protestants, Orthodox, and Roman Catholics all shared Eucharist. It was a genuine Christian union accompanied by vibrant music.

Three years later, the Faith and Order Commission met in Moshi, Tanzania, a small town that lies at the foot of Mount Kilimanjaro. The beautiful scenery contrasted with the poorness of the town, whose roads were filled with potholes and water puddles. I remember one Western participant saying, "This is the Africa I have always wanted to see." That did not amuse the African participants, who felt this was a situation where the health and wellbeing of the townspeople were being neglected.

Unfortunately, this same young woman went out to see the sunrise the next morning, slipped, and broke her ankle in one of the same ditches that we knew meant no one was keeping up the roads. The local hospital put a cast on her ankle and we all signed it, as a memento of her visit. Perhaps she learned something about whether the Africa she saw was the one that should be the Africa that one could imagine.

Theologically, both the Spain and Tanzania gatherings broadened my global perspective as to how worldwide Christendom is engaged to promote the good news. It helped us to understand how similar our problems were around the world. We went home with the mandate to confess our faith in Jesus Christ as the core values of mission and evangelism in worldwide Christendom.

PRESIDENT OF THE ZIMBABWE COUNCIL OF CHURCHES

Soon after I was elected as Bishop of Manicaland in 1999, I was elected President of the Zimbabwe Council of Churches. The Council consisted of twenty-one heads of various denominations and was a decidedly mixed bag of church leaders: ultra-conservatives, moderates, liberals, and a few extreme left members. But by and large, the majority were diehard members of ZANU(PF), attempting to serve both God and Caesar. One of those diehards was Norbert Kunonga, who I would clash with later in my life.

As President of the Council, it was considered taboo to issue a public statement on issues like violence or corruption without first consulting each of the twenty-one members. For me, this was a ridiculous custom; I found I couldn't remain silent in the face of atrocities that were being committed against innocent people. But the majority of ZANU(PF) supporters didn't want to be at odds with their party, so the Council's leadership stayed silent. They were caught in the nets of hypocrisy and pretended as if nothing was happening. So, when I issued a statement at the Annual General Meeting condemning violence in our nation, I became very unpopular.

Some bishops were attacked by their church members saying they shouldn't have allowed me to make that statement, arguing that the Council should have nothing to do with politics; something I never accepted. The head of one denomination—a lawyer who lost his license in a corruption probe—immediately called for an extraordinary executive meeting to oust me as President; a proposal that was rejected. But the campaign against my leadership continued and, at the next Annual General Meeting, I was voted out as President.

There is always a price to pay in serving the people but for me, this one was good. To serve the people of God for me is to condemn perpetrators of injustice against the powerless, as a way of encouraging them not to be pushed into despair, disillusion, and hopelessness. Yet it was also a reminder that to be called to serve people is a call to walk on a very rough and dangerous road.

Though Kunonga wasn't usually a regular participant at Council meetings, he made sure to attend the meeting where my continued service as President was up for a vote. He came with his wife, who, although she was not a delegate, was allowed to cast her vote; a small, but telling example of how corrupt the whole process was. The disbarred lawyer, who gave himself the title of bishop, backed Kunonga.

Being no longer curtailed by my position as President, I was so happy to feel free to speak my mind. As a bishop of the Diocese of Manicaland, I remained on the Council as the head of a denomination, but I now felt free of censorship to speak up for the powerless.

Corruption was affecting every sector in our nation and we were starved for a prophetic voice from the Council. Yet, the Council leadership opted not to be consistent with the mission of the church. On my part I remained hopeful that sooner or later the Council would follow in the footsteps of its founding fathers, Reverend Ndhlela and Bishop Skelton, who were courageous church leaders with prophetic voices against the oppressive and racist white settler regime. The Council had been founded to be a prophetic voice against a regime oppressing black people. The founders could not turn a blind eye or have their ears unstopped to hear the voices of those crying in police and prison cells in restricted camps. The Council needed to be reminded again and again that it was not an arm of the government but a missionary agent, listening to the voice of Jesus commissioning his disciples saying "You go to all the nations and baptize them in the name of the Father and of the Son and the Holy Spirit" (Matthew 28:19).

CHAPTER SIXTEEN

Zimbabwe – A Polarized Country

The year 2006—shortly before my retirement as Bishop of Manicaland—was a memorable one. For one, my laptop was stolen while Rut, Nyasha, and Tinao were visiting our dear friends, the Waetjens, in Berkeley. Herman Waetjens and his dear wife had been great friends of ours when we were first in Berkeley, and, again, when I returned to finish my doctorate in 1991.

I remember the theft of my laptop so clearly because it symbolized, in some ways, the way Zimbabwe, sixteen years after its first free elections, was still a polarized nation, something I got to see close-up as the leader of a reconciliation team.

This team had been brought together to try to reconcile Robert Mugabe, then President of Zimbabwe, and his political rival Morgan Tsvangirai. Tsvangirai and his supporters accused Mugabe of stealing the election and refused to recognize him as the chosen leader of the nation. I was, at that time, Bishop of the Diocese of Manicaland and President of the Zimbabwe Council of Churches.

I was astonished that Mugabe, the man I once supported while I was in exile, the former Marxist, now owned fifteen big farms. Once, you could have a dialogue with him; now, nobody dared question or contradict him. He didn't even bother to attend the negotiations but delegated them to lieutenants—an action that indicated his unwillingness to take them seriously.

During the negotiations, that break-in and theft of my laptop occurred. I had a suspicion that it wasn't a garden-variety burglary, partly because when I called the police, they came immediately. That was unusual.

And I never heard from them again—it has been more than fifteen years and I am still waiting for the promised return of my laptop! I suspected that the robbers were looking for confidential information. Unfortunately for them, all they found were a series of sermons on Matthew 23, which is all about Jesus' calling out of the hypocrites of his time.

The mandate of our negotiations was to try and bring the two protagonists to the same table to talk. Tsvangirai was willing but Mugabe could not be persuaded to face Tsvangirai; that was delegated to three senior members of ZANU(PF): Vice President John Nkomo, Dr. Nathan Shamuyarira, who was a Senior Member of the ZANU Central Committee, and General Chiwewe, the Governor of Masvingo. Mugabe's basic directive to his team was to get Tsvangirai to accept him as Head of State, clearly a way to simply buy time. Mugabe was trying to use us as a mere post office service, to deliver messages to Tsvangirai from his side.

We told Mugabe's team that we were interested only in true reconciliation; that we were there to bring Tsvangirai and Mugabe together, so as to reach a mutual recognition of each other's position, and to remove the polarization that was preventing the nation from moving forward. But Mugabe's team, seasoned ZANU(PF) politicians, were trying to play us for fools, and, indeed, they were successful in keeping us from seeing Mugabe and having him come to sit down and truly negotiate.

I remained amazed at how different the man I met years ago in Germany had changed; how power had corrupted him. When he came to West Germany, we talked with him face to face as you would any other person, and he shared our frustration about the slow pace of our liberation movement. Now, consumed by power, everything had changed about him—his appearance, mannerisms, eyes, ears, hands, face, voice, and gestures—they were all used to display an outward expression of power and unwillingness to give up any of that power. His long-hidden agenda to attain absolute power had now been achieved. Absolute power had consumed him; he was no longer the same man I had known, just a shadow of who he was in the past.

But some good came out of serving on that reconciliation team, at least for me, personally. I became closer to the Roman Catholic Bishop Patrick Musume. I remember Patrick saying to me, "Sebastian, what Zimbabwe needs now is God's intervention and that is your task and mine to pray for that to happen." My brother, Patrick, was to me not just a Roman Catholic Bishop, but a true brother in Christ, as I was to him. Patrick transcended denominational walls which separated many would-be brothers and sisters in Christ.

Reconciliation remains a national challenge in Zimbabwe to this day. Our politicians are engaged in fighting against each other instead of fighting for national development. I still live in hope that my native land will one day have rulers who believe that everybody counts; where peace and justice are experienced by all citizens regardless of social status; where even enemies are reconciled to each other.

Before we served on the reconciliation committee, I had been asked by Bishop Patrick and Bishop Muchabaiwa to preach at the Roman Catholic Cathedral in Mutare at the memorial service of Pope John Paul II. I was touched and humbled by this brotherly gesture from the bishops. The service was attended by Christians from all denominations in and around Mutare. We gave thanks to God for the gift he had given His church in the person of Pope John Paul II.

Bishop Patrick was a great reconciler. When he was taken ill Rut and I took turns to go and pray with him every week. In the course of our weekly prayers together, he said to me, "Sebastian, I would like you to preach at my funeral should I die before you." My response to him was, "Yes, and I would like you to do the same if I go before you." Unfortunately, he will not preach at mine, but I did fulfill his wish.

This is what I think of when I think of my good friend:

Yes, Patrick.
So, brief a life and then endless death,
so, a brief life, and then endless peace and justice.
Love, you gave it to your people in Zimbabwe by showing courage amidst danger.
You were faithful to your vocation and remained steadfast to the end.
You never sold your spiritual birthright like other church leaders or pastors for a green dollar or a bond note.
Your legacy remains in our memories, yesterday, today, and tomorrow.
Your commitment to the core values of the Gospel, Peace, and Justice remains a landmark of your short-lived life.
The struggle for power, money, and politics in our nation rages on without an end in sight, just like it was before you passed on.
We are where you left us.
Rest in Peace my good friend; rest in God's Hands.

Rut is gone and so is Patrick. I miss both of them. May they rest eternally and peacefully in the place where we shall all be called when it's time for us to take our place in His Eternal Glory.

We still long for leadership that truly understands genuine democracy. What we have now in our country is a lip-service democracy still undermined largely by clannism, tribalism, and regionalism. No freedom, no equal rights, no nationhood yet—true democracy is absent. Educated as we think we are, we have to learn from our neighbors across the borders; they understand the principles of democracy much better than we do.

Zimbabwe needs a new generation of politicians who can redeem the situation. I do not doubt in my mind that God is not indifferent to the needs of the oppressed people of Zimbabwe. The stony-hearted liberation leadership will not be there forever; God will provide the nation with a leader who will have people at his or her heart.

CHAPTER SEVENTEEN

Expansion of the Mothers Union and a New Health Center

While I was Bishop of Manicaland, there were two projects Rut and I saw to fruition that I felt were especially in response to the special needs of the people of the diocese and Zimbabwe. The first was the expansion of the Mothers Union in Manicaland. The second was the establishment of a new health center in an area that desperately needed medical services for people living in far-flung rural areas.

MOTHERS' UNION IN MANICALAND

While I was involved in organizing evangelism and mission efforts and tending to the needs of the diocese, Rut became very involved with supporting the Mothers' Union—a guild of the Anglican Church that had about 3,000 members in the diocese. Women formed the backbone of the church in Manicaland, as many of the men had to be away in the big cities to earn a living to support their families. As a theologian and educator, Rut organized a series of leadership training sessions for branch leaders in every district who she later commissioned to go and teach congregation about the important role of mothers in their families and communities. Thus, she was able to convey her passion for teaching to others, so they could go out and teach more women.

The Mothers' Union is a worldwide organization in the Anglican Communion. It plays a major role in ministry, especially through its members visiting the sick, comforting bereaved families, and doing other works of charity. Unfortunately, in some dioceses, some diocesan bishops have taken over the Mothers' Union and ignored their place as an autonomous organization, with its own constitution that gave them the power to run their own affairs. The courses that Rut developed were meant to empower women so that they would gain confidence as role models and substantive lay members of their congregations.

When training sessions were completed in all the districts, Rut called for a Mothers' Union convention in August 2000. More than 3,000 members attended the convention held at St. Augustine's Mission, Penhalonga. It was very moving to witness this huge crowd of women who had traveled long distances to commit themselves to the work of the Union. Even though Manicaland is a poor diocese, these women had paid for their transportation to be at the five-day convention. This was quite an undertaking in the organization, including feeding such a huge crowd. The Union, however, had raised enough money for the conference. A white farmer in the neighborhood donated beef from three of his animals to the convention.

Although St. Augustine's Church could seat 700 people, it proved too small for the 3,000 delegates, so two huge tents were erected to accommodate the rest of the participants. Loudspeakers made it possible for all to worship together.

Seeing that assembly convinced me that the people of Manicaland, though poor in worldly goods, were spiritually rich. I could also see that there was real potential for the diocese to become self-sustaining. Following Rut's leadership, participants proposed an annual conference where social issues affecting women would be discussed. Experts, such as lawyers, would be invited to inform mothers about issues like inheritance laws that affected so many widows who were often taken advantage of by members of the extended family. Another very difficult issue that needed discussion were questions about child abuse. Before the conference that Rut organized, the Union was mostly concerned with things like fashion and choir competitions; Rut believed it was more important for women to talk about issues that affected their well-being and the well-being of their families and communities.

Rut had a personal touch that drew people to her. Mothers' Union members saw her not as a white woman but as one of them. She was able to put into practice her faith and action. As her Mothers' Union partner Sue Stringham, who was from Northampton in the U.K., and president of the organization, said at Rut's memorial service, "Rut will live on in the hearts of many people for a long time. I do not think that many people who knew her will easily forget her; she was unique. I miss hearing her voice; yes, it was through her letters and written words she described so vividly her thoughts and her feelings, what she had done and what she felt she should have done—that it was as if she was speaking in that clear decisive voice which persuaded us all that she was right."

Rut was a good listener and an unassuming person. She accepted all people regardless of their social status and they felt comfortable in her presence. She encouraged women to be themselves by standing up for their rights and place in the church. Though some clergy resented women's leadership, the women were unstoppable because they are in the majority in the church. Because of who Rut was, people did not think about her skin color; she simply became one of them. She had a fantastic memory, always remembering everyone's name. That was invaluable for me, as I've always had a poor memory. At social gatherings, I would wait to hear her greet people, so I would learn their names. Now that she is no more, my poor memory has been exposed. What a helpful companion she was to me in our ministry. A call to serve people can be very hard and challenging, but through Rut, and her ministry in the Mothers' Union, I felt my pastoral wings were spread wider.

One of the things I learned, in the many years of my ministry, is that a call to serve the people of God is a collective response. Jesus had more than twelve disciples: "The harvest is plentiful but the workers are few" (Matthew 9:37). To serve the Diocese of Manicaland was to respond to the call to serve God's people and to preach the Good News in various ways. That was not just a task for the ordained, but also the laity. Much of the mission and evangelism work is done by women who visit the sick, comfort grieving families, and encourage each other in times of personal or family crisis.

NEW HEALTH CENTER

The province of Manicaland, although endowed with mineral and agricultural resources, is one of the poorest provinces in the country. Still, it has a hallowed place in our nation's history. Because it shares a national boundary with Mozambique it was often used as an escape route for the freedom fighters who would then attack Rhodesia from Mozambique. An unknown number of freedom fighters were killed around the Mozambique town of

Chimoio, which lies some 60 kilometers from the Zimbabwe border. There is a cemetery where freedom fighters were buried that is now a landmark. Mugabe himself escaped from Rhodesia to Mozambique.

One striking feature I noticed as I began my travels in the diocese after being elected Bishop, was that Manicaland Province lagged in development compared to other provinces, and especially there was an absence of health centers in many rural districts. Even the few mission hospitals were miles apart from each other.

On one of my pastoral visits, I was near one of the few clinics when I met two elderly women who were bringing another woman, their relative, to this clinic that was 18 kilometers away from their village. The sick woman could not walk and so, with no other means of transport, they had pushed her in a wheelbarrow. This must have been a journey of some hours for these elderly women. It reminded me of the story in Luke's gospel when Jesus heals the paralytic (Luke 5:17-39); it made me so sad to think about what they had to go through because of a lack of health centers.

As I continued with my pastoral journey, the image of the woman in a wheelbarrow was stuck in my mind. I started questioning why the church, after so many years, had not focused as much on the ministry to the sick as they had on education. The diocese had built so many primary and secondary schools, but only one hospital. And so many people in the rural and impoverished areas died from diseases like malaria because they lacked medical care. I decided that one of my mission challenges during my tenure would be to establish health centers to help eliminate disease and reduce the long distances to health centers.

As for the sick woman I saw that day, I learned later that she had passed on in that wheelbarrow, as her relatives were pushing her back home. It was likely that the rural clinic staff couldn't deal with whatever illness she was suffering from, and there was no ambulance to take her to the nearest hospital, which was about 40 kilometers away. So, the women who brought her to the health center had no choice but to take her back home. It was a very sad story and one that was repeated all over our country.

At my first synod meeting, I told the story of the woman in the wheelbarrow to the delegates. I said, only partly joking, that they should avoid being taken ill or else they also might very well die in a wheelbarrow.

On another trip after a confirmation service in a rural congregation that was situated along a hilltop range, I gave a lift home to an old lady. I asked her where she would go for medical treatment if she fell ill.

"I would die!" she replied. "There are no clinics around here; the nearest clinic is beyond those hills over there," she said, pointing to some hills far away from where we were towards the border with Mozambique. "Our member of parliament comes to this area only at the time of elections; he does not care about us!" she continued. Abject poverty and diseases are the major enemies of the people in Manicaland province.

By chance, after that conversation, I officiated at a wedding ceremony of a couple related to the member of parliament who the old woman said didn't care about his district. I asked him whether he had plans to have a health center in his area and he claimed that plans were underway to build more health centers in the province. But Zimbabwe became independent in 1980; here we were twenty-two years later and the situation had not changed.

Because of those experiences, I reminded members of my executive council that healing was one of the major tasks of the ministry of the church; a ministry which we had seriously neglected. Jesus spent a lot of his ministry healing the sick—his works of mercy towards the sick ought to inspire us, I told them. I was determined to build a clinic in one of those neglected areas.

To construct health centers is a huge undertaking. I would need good and generous people to come forward, people with compassion who were prepared to be involved in such kinds of works of mercy. Manicaland, like any other province in the country, is frequently visited by ambassadors, mainly from the Western governments, who are taken around on what is known as "familiarization tours." That was something I could perhaps do—appeal to a foreign dignitary on one of those tours.

The first person that came by while I was considering this move was the British High Commissioner, Brian Donnelly. During his official tour in the province, he came to see me at our diocesan office. I told him my story and the kind of challenges I was facing in our impoverished province. I was not asking for a donation but sharing my stories with him. He was a good listener and very sympathetic.

After listening to my stories, he said, "I am going to assist with the building of the health center." I was stunned with disbelief, so much so, that I thought I had gone deaf and did not hear what he just said. When I finally understood his words, I didn't have the right words to respond with—he must have noticed that it took the breath right out of me!

Donnelly went on to say that he would share the idea of building a health center with the Dutch Ambassador Wettering, who he said was a gracious man. Four years later, when the health center became a reality, both were no longer in Zimbabwe, so the Australian ambassador represented them at its opening.

We identified the village of Nhedziwa as a central place, with a large population, as the best location for the new health center. The Makoni District Council offered us a sizable piece of land and also provided us with standard plans for a clinic from the Ministry of Construction. We sat down with the villagers to discuss in earnest the importance of the clinic and how the community could contribute toward its general welfare. The British and the Dutch embassies funded the construction of the main building and, in addition, three staff houses.

The next donor to come on board was the Australian Ambassador, Matthew Neuhaus, whose contributions exceeded my expectations, including connecting the clinic to electricity, which involved running a line from the main supply line, about half a kilometer away, and constructing a maternity ward, including the furnishings. Though our government had basic requirements for rural clinics, they didn't include a maternity ward. In our case, the maternity ward was in response to the requests of the community. Some mothers never made it to a clinic when they were due to deliver, while others arrived at the last hour when they were desperate if there was a problem. Now, with a maternity ward at the clinic, expectant mothers could stay for several months before their due date. The ward was very popular because it released expectant mothers from chores at home that give them no time to rest during the last stages of pregnancy.

The three foreign missions were instrumental in the establishment of our Nedziwe Center—one of the best health centers in the province. Patients, including expectant mothers, came from beyond the boundaries we originally envisioned because of the excellent medical care. This was yet another service offered by men of goodwill; foreign diplomats with a mission to serve the needy.

Rut sat down with the local people and their chief and formed a management committee. She talked to them about what it meant for them to have a health center in their community, and what role they should play. The community contributed building materials such as sand, concrete stones, and bricks. Contributing building materials gave them a sense of ownership and it got them away from the dependency syndrome which has become a national disease. The clinic management committee was formed to run and maintain the clinic. In a province that is so impoverished, teaching people to be self-reliant by embarking on sustainable projects is a necessity.

A call to serve people has several fronts. As a church, the Anglican Church was one of the pioneers in the country to introduce formal education and did very well in this sector by building numerous schools in the diocese. But health service delivery hadn't been their strong point. We have overlooked or neglected a major component of the mission of the church. We need more clinics in the Diocese to help eliminate preventable diseases. My goal as the Bishop of the Diocese was to revisit our missionary agenda in the diocese to preach, teach—through formal education—and provide healing facilities with clinics and hospitals. We have to remind ourselves that healing the sick was one of the major components of Jesus' proclamation of the gospel; sadly, that doesn't feature regularly in our weekly services anymore, even when we know the faithful are still yearning for spiritual healing.

When I conducted a healing service during the Mother's Union Conference at St. Augustine's Mission, the participants seemed exhausted by the day-long conference, so I chose a side chapel, out of the way, for the few people I assumed would want this service. But it turned out that almost the whole packed church wanted to heal—everybody wanted me to lay their hands on them! It was like they were crashing a party as they tried to get through the chapel gates—but what they were yearning for was God's grace. The following day, I was told that some women came twice and so they got a double share of the healing grace of God! The gate-crashing was a clear message to me as a bishop that healing was very much needed in our ministry.

For the faithful, there is no difference between spiritual and physical healing. Though I caution that a healing service is not an addendum to the Eucharist; it is a separate service altogether. The Lord's Supper offers us both spiritual and physical healing; in this sacrament, we encounter Jesus, the healer of our bodies and souls. The Eucharist is not like a supermarket where you pick up one item and then go back for another. That is why I believe a healing service should not be offered directly after the Eucharist service as though they are the same thing. In the Sacrament of Eucharist, we encounter and receive Jesus himself the Great Healer of our physical and spiritual needs. A healing service can be important but not as a mere addendum to the Eucharist liturgy proper.

* * *

The official opening of the clinic was a grand event for the local community. Chief and headmen and their people graced the occasion. I felt honored to preach to a congregation of people who had very little to do with the church because I felt that they too would be able to hear the good news of Jesus' works of mercy. I said to them that the community had suffered for a long time from diseases like malaria and bilharzia, as well as a lack of medication for those with chronic illnesses. The clinic was now in their midst to offer such a service. After the church service was over and there were introductions of guests by the clinic chief's spokesperson, I introduced two government officials from the ministry of health. Last, but not least, I had the privilege to introduce His Excellency the Ambassador of Australia, Matthew Neuhaus, and his wife Angela. The Embassy had played such a major role in the construction of the clinic.

Nhedziwa Clinic is surrounded by several villages and about five hundred people had gathered for the official opening ceremony. Some people had not seen an ambassador in their community and so that was a big draw. Though Matthew and Angela may have seemed exotic to the villagers, as the Ambassador was an active Anglican layman, his knowledge of rural Zimbabwe was profound. He had been to every part of the province and had seen the needs of the rural and impoverished people.

As I watched such a huge crowd gathering for the clinic's official opening, I began to worry whether there was enough food to feed everyone at a planned reception. What Rut and I didn't know was that those weeks before the event, a local committee had organized a catering group because word had gotten around that the bishop had invited an ambassador to come and officially open the clinic. An anonymous villager donated a steer, and two other well-wishers donated a goat apiece. Chickens, fresh and dried vegetables, tomatoes, and peanuts were donated by members of the catering group. Food was prepared by a retired hotel chef and it was a good feast. Although the Ambassador and his wife had attended similar occasions elsewhere, they didn't expect such an extensive menu presented by the rural poor of Manicaland. I remember saying to Matthew and Angela that the poorer people are, the more generous they become. It is in sharing the little they have that God cares for their daily needs. Our special guests and a few other people were served a local drink called *Maheu* which is made out of cooked cornmeal with a little sugar and ground *rapoko*—a type of millet— and allowed to ferment overnight. Though it's fermented, it's nonalcoholic, and so is enjoyed by adults and children alike.

The Ambassador gave a touching speech about how this long-awaited health center was here to help the community eliminate curable diseases and also to reduce infant and maternal mortality. For the first time, villagers saw that foreign embassies were offering more services to them than their government.

What I found most satisfying about this project was not only the number of generous donors we had, but also the contributions from the local community, not only in material, but also in their labor, by carrying sand, stone, and water to the construction site. That collective response gave the individuals a sense of ownership of the clinic and also of being able to serve one another for the betterment of all. My thanks also were to Rut who had tirelessly spent time teaching people in the community how to take ownership of their health center.

But above all, the church was carrying out its mission to heal the sick in their community; without this kind of assistance, the community would have been without a clinic within a realistic commuting distance. In addition to the Nhedziwa Clinic, we also converted an unfinished building to be a clinic at St. Mary's Magdalene in the Nyanga District. We also renovated an abandoned building St. Webster Mission. It was all in service to the belief that the ministry of healing has to play a significant role in the church.

CHAPTER EIGHTEEN

Mutare, Our Earthly Home

As a very young child, my associations with the city of Mutare were negative, because it's where my grandmother died in hospital in 1948. But when I was older, I made frequent visits to Mutare and I came to love it, mostly because of its scenery. Mutare is surrounded by mountains offering breathtaking panoramic views to rich and poor alike. The mountains are shaped like a crater, with the city in its center, making for stunning vistas.

Eventually, Mutare became my favorite city—in the world, even. When I was living in Europe and the United States, I always had Mutare's beauty in mind. When you live in Mutare, you cannot help but admire the beauty of God's creation. Each day is different. Sometimes mist mostly covers the mountains; other days, the mountains stand forth clearly against blue skies. The one disadvantage of Mutare's location is that the mountains are prone to lightning strikes that can be so intense that, every year, people are killed during electrical storms. Once, when I was sitting in my study with the window open, a lightning bolt came through and almost hit me!

Yet, when one sits, as Rut and I used to do quietly at our home in Mutare, viewing the panoramic worldview so visibly placed in front of us, you are reminded constantly of the awesome beauty of God's creation.

When we returned to Zimbabwe after independence, even after we owned a house in Mount Pleasant, we looked to buy a stand in Mutare. (A stand in Africa means the same thing as a plot of land owned by the deed-holder.) We were on a waiting list for a long time, from 1984 to 2000; I had to make some noise because we were waiting so long. Eventually, when the Mutare City Council offered us the stand, I went to see it with the city surveyor. Rut was still in Harare, so I asked her to come to Mutare for the weekend to view the land.

When she came, we went up to see it together. It was situated on a small hilltop, a hectare stand covered with stones—which was one of the reasons nobody wanted to build on it. But Rut and I loved it because of the wonderful views.

Since we were married, we had moved three times to Germany and three times to Zimbabwe. All of our houses had architectural features that we liked, and those we didn't. Surely, we thought, having all those experiences of living in houses of different shapes and sizes, we could sit down and design the features of our dream house. When we finished our unprofessional design, we handed our draft to an architect who simply said that there was nothing more to add except dimensions. We had the town engineer design and build the columns for our main verandah; we even had a second verandah at the back of the kitchen that provides some warmth from the sun during the winter months. The main verandah is accessed through French doors. It offers a panoramic view of the city of Mutare and its mountain range which is about 60-to-70 kilometers away. There is a swimming pool that also overlooks that same vista. There is an unusual beauty to the sunsets one can watch from the verandah; it is different each day.

But our dream house on top of the hill didn't come without a lot of effort and cost. For one thing, the huge stones that had deterred other potential owners had to be removed before the building could begin. An earthmover would cost $250 per hour—much more than Rut and I ever had. Even selling our Mount Pleasant house—something we did with regret as we loved it, and the girls considered it home—didn't give us enough money to meet that kind of construction cost. And as we tried to figure out how we could afford the boulder removal, building materials costs were going up by the day. At the time we had a home in the official Bishop's residence but that would no longer be available when I retired. And our children were very nervous about where we would go upon retirement.

And then, once again, we experienced God's providence, like we had had before in Berkeley when Bishop Mallory came to us with provisions when my stipend had not yet arrived. This time it was a family friend, Jimmy Khatso, who was then the director of the Zimbabwe National Water Authority. He offered us an earthmover, only asking me to buy a 44 gallon-drum of diesel, which we gladly did. The job was done in eighteen hours.

The hilltop was divided in the middle to create a platform for the lower garden with plenty of space for a lawn and swimming pool. The other half of the stand would provide enough space for an orchard, and a flower and vegetable garden. Thank you, Jimmy, and your wife, Dorothy, for appearing on the scene to redeem us at a time when we thought we might end up with no house at all.

Fortunately, just at the time we were ready to move forward with construction, Rut was working for the Border Timber Company, so we could use her employee discount for much of the material for our new house. With Rut's discount, the money we got from selling our house now could go a long way. It took us three years to finish the project. We did have some problems—construction workers sometimes stole material from the site and sold it. Though eventually they were arrested, each loss was still a setback.

Church people and their clergy who come from other countries often didn't understand why we needed to build a house for our retirement—surely my service in the church would leave me well taken care of? And I often tell them this story: I once went to one of the homesteads for a funeral of a well-known and respected senior priest, who had done so much in the service of God and had become a leader in the church. The only house he owned was a tiny round hut in his village, a house with no windows, where he and his wife lived after his retirement. It had a narrow door at the entrance, so narrow that the undertakers could not manage to put the casket in the hut. They had to remove the door frames so that the casket could rest on the floor. There was only a small space for one priest; the rest of the clergy stood outside the hut.

It brought home forcefully the differences in the different parts of Anglicanism. British missionaries working overseas have retirement provisions for them which include medical aid, a retirement home, or a livable pension. African priests had no meaningful retirement benefits let alone a decent place to retire. On retirement, it was common for an African clergyman to return to his rural home and to live in very poor accommodations unless he had made provisions for a decent home after retirement. I felt so happy that we had made a good decision to have our own house. I would not have wanted to expose my family to such a situation.

When the house was finished, Rut took care of the interior decoration while my job was to tend to landscaping the garden—a job that required four levels of terraces on the rocky hill. Luckily, I found a gardener who was very skillful at the stonework.

We divided the garden into a vegetable garden, orchard, a space for a lawn, a pool, and a chapel. When the layout of the garden was finished and we were ready to move in, our dream house was more than we had imagined. I planted fruit trees in the orchards: plums, avocado, pawpaw, pear, orange, lemon trees, and three types of banana plants including plantains. Nyasha planted mango trees. Though my responsibility was the exterior portions, Ruth helped design the pool and did a splendid job. Around the pool are assorted bushes including Japanese maple and palms. The garden includes a collection of exotic flowers from California's Marin County, from Germany's Heidelberg, and a rosemary bush from the south of France. Having a garden like ours makes me always want to buy different kinds of flower seeds whenever I come across beautiful, unusual kinds in a nursery.

Our dream house changed our practice of forever moving around from one place to another because the idea of having a permanent home was so fulfilling. We were now old and needed to have a place to rest and serve the diocese living in our own home. I was so grateful to Rut, my companion, partner, friend, and my wife, who, like the biblical Ruth, was always ready to move on when we were younger. Now, indeed, we had reached our last destination where we hoped to grow old together.

We even had a surprise visit a short time after we moved in after my retirement as Bishop of Manicaland in 2006. It was from an Austrian solar technician who was installing solar equipment in church hospitals and clinics. He said that he had some left-over equipment he did not want to take back to Harare; would we mind if he installed solar heating for the main house and at our caretaker's house? We readily welcomed the idea, although we were not familiar with solar heating technology. The nice man did a good job; it has functioned so well to date since its installation and helped us to reduce the hot water bill, and we have since connected it to help power our lights, our television, and refrigerators.

Of course, when our granddaughter Nomsa came to visit, she called our pool a pond, because, as an American, she was used to much larger pools. Nevertheless, our pool was where she learned to swim and dive well.

We built a traditional round chapel on the property in memory of our parents, Eunice and Eric Bakare and Magdalena and Hans Büchsel—their names are engraved on a slate that hangs in the chapel. In this small chapel, Rut and I held our morning and evening prayers, which I still do. This is a place and a time to make intercessions for our family and friends, far and near. I continue to pray for peace and justice in our broken world, for genuine love among people regardless of color or cultural differences. In my evening prayers, I continue to pray for Zimbabwe, for freedom and human rights, for the persecuted, oppressed, the sick and hungry, and those without shelter.

I had hoped to grow old alongside Rut at our home, but that was not to be. My dear wife is no longer with me in this life, but she is with me in spirit. She is now resting in eternal peace in the place we shall all go. It's very hard for me to think of moving away from this house, and especially the chapel, a place of spiritual connection with those who have gone before us. I see Rut and her decorative skills in every corner of the house. She is very much present and I cannot separate myself from her. Although her chair in the chapel is now empty, sometimes, I sit in my chair silently and I feel her praying, as she always did. As a retired Bishop Emeritus, I am sometimes away, serving the diocese through prayers and preaching. I also travel to Harare to visit my daughter Tinao and her husband Julius. Every year, I try to travel to the United States to visit Nyasha, her husband Allan, and my granddaughter Nyasha in New Jersey. And there are plans, eventually, to visit my daughter Rufaro in Frankfurt, as well as an upcoming wedding that Rufaro and her fiancé are planning. But Mutare remains my home and I always look forward to returning. I am glad that our children share the same sentiments about the house Rut and I built.

CHAPTER NINETEEN

A Caretaker Bishop

After my retirement as diocesan bishop of Manicaland, I was offered a lectureship at Africa University in the Department of Theology to teach Systematic Theology and Professional Ethics.

My retirement as Bishop of Manicaland at age 65 had not been entirely my own choice as I hoped to retiree three years later. The main reason for being forced to retire was that when I was still Bishop of the Diocese of Manicaland I had sponsored a motion supporting the ordination of women as deacons in the church at the Provincial Synod for the Church of the Province of Central Africa that was being held in Malawi. The ordination of women had been approved by some dioceses in the province including Zimbabwe, Botswana, and three dioceses in Zambia. The only dioceses which did not accept women's ordination were Malawi and the Lusaka diocese in Zambia. The Archbishop at that time, Bernard Malango, was dead set against women's ordination. I naively counted on the newly ordained younger bishops to support my motion but they developed cold feet and voted against my resolution. I was amazed at the sheer hypocrisy of those who had promised to support my motion in private and then voted against it. From then on, I was viewed as someone likely to be a bad influence on the youthful bishops, so the Archbishop wanted to get rid of me from the episcopate. I even went so far as to speak up and say that the Archbishop's leadership was void of vision and that the Province of Central Africa lacked understanding of the dynamic power of the Spirit in the Church and her call to do mission and evangelism in the twenty-first century. And the arguments that they came up with against my motion were so archaic.

Things like—Jesus was not a woman, so, therefore, we cannot have women priests—I simply could not accept that kind of retrograde reasoning.

Besides the fight over women's ordination, the other Zimbabwean bishops were generally not very happy with me, because I continually asked them to condemn the rampant violence and other forms of injustices perpetrated by the Mugabe regime. They were petrified of issuing a collective statement that would openly condemn the unjust practices of the regime. To let me carry on with my episcopacy in Manicaland would mean exposing their silence. It was the bishops of Zimbabwe who especially wanted to see me retire.

So, after my retirement, when I was invited to lecture at Africa University, I felt as though I had reached a safe way to do mission and evangelism through theological education. The one drawback was that the classes were very large and it was hard to give students individual attention. But the faculty had plans to hire a second lecturer and I was looking forward to the smaller classes. As soon as they did, however, I received another call to go back into one of the most difficult situations I faced as a shepherd of God's people: To be a caretaker Bishop in the Diocese of Harare that had been torn apart by Nolbert Kunonga.

* * *

Some background on the Diocese of Harare is called for here. The Diocese of Harare was originally founded by Bishop George Knight-Bruce in 1891. He was a missionary from Britain, sent by The Society for the Propagation of the Gospel in Foreign Parts. This was a High Church missionary organization of the Church of England whose responsibility was to recruit bishops to serve newly-formed dioceses in other lands. But as there was no desire to develop African leadership in the church, those bishops at that time weren't African. The missionary-led Anglican church did not foresee that one day the British settler-colonial leadership would be replaced by Africans. When that happened in the 1980s, they didn't have African priests with the kind of graduate theological education that priests had in England to provide comparable leadership. By the time I became Bishop, however, some African priests had the kind of education in theology and leadership that was needed for the church in the newly independent countries.

But in 2007, Kunonga, who was then the Bishop of the Diocese of Harare, hadn't been trained at an Anglican seminary and essentially had no theological or ministerial formation. What he had was the support of

President Mugabe, who hoped he would deliver votes from the diocese to support Zanu(PF) in the 2005 elections. To their utter humiliation, the opposition party, the Movement for Democratic Change, won.

At the time, Kunonga was trying to split the diocese off from the Anglican Communion. Kunonga was a power-hungry, ambitious bishop who wanted to become the Archbishop of the new church province he was planning to create. He planned to call it the Province of Anglican National Church in Zimbabwe. The Province of Central Africa had resisted and there was an ongoing fight over the church properties—not unlike the court battles in the United States between the Episcopal Church and the breakaway Anglican Church in North America. The new Archbishop approached me on behalf of the Church of the Province of Central Africa and asked me to be the caretaker bishop of the Diocese of Harare. When I asked why there wasn't a single sitting bishop who was prepared to take on the role, I was told that they were too afraid of Mugabe. I accepted, not because the bishops asked me, but because I realized that it was my call to put my life into a den of lions. If it was a "call to serve my people," I was happy to take it. I would do my best to serve the church and God himself would do the rest.

The first thing I did after my appointment as caretaker bishop was to call all those who were against Kunonga to ask them to meet me in a hotel in Harare because all church facilities were being held by Kunonga and his accomplices. I was disheartened when only nineteen people responded to my invitation, but I tried again, issuing a second invitation for a meeting at St. Michael's in Mbare, a church where the rector had openly opposed Kunonga. This time, a huge crowd turned up. We could say that, what Kunonga's supporters were describing as a remnant was, actually, the majority of church members.

We all agreed to elect delegates to fill all the necessary diocesan committees from those who were present, as well as others who couldn't attend in person who were known to be against Kunonga. We were ready to function as a diocese, even without money and church buildings. The faithful chose to meet in houses or the open. We not only had the majority of the dioceses' committed lay people, but we also had a few courageous priests among us. Their slogan was "We are CPCA." The Diocese of Harare in the Church Province of Central Africa came back to life!

By then, Kunonga had been excommunicated by the church authorities. But he and Mugabe started a propaganda war against the CPCA, claiming that we were a "colonial church," because of our relationship to the Church of England through the Anglican Communion, and that we had no place in an independent Zimbabwe. Mugabe also enlisted the head of the national police force, Augustine Chihuri, to have his men harass and intimidate CPCA members.

Every Sunday morning Chihuri deployed a police force to guard all the churches, preventing CPCA members from using their church buildings. I recommended members organize so-called church houses, a practice used by the early church when Christians were being persecuted by the Roman emperor Nero. It worked. Meetings in houses drew huge crowds of people including the lapsed or backsliders who were angry because they felt their church was being attacked by police. One old man was heard saying, "I was born and raised in this church and I am ready to die for it. What have the police to do with us?"

While we were barred from using our church buildings, the police continued to guard our empty church buildings as if they were guarding our property against thieves' break-ins. The congregation of the Cathedral of St. Mary's and All Saints met at the Less Brown public swimming pool for their Sunday services. The Bishop of Massachusetts, Tom Shaw, preached a moving sermon to the congregation gathered around the pool and the police were among those who cheered together with the congregants! Meanwhile, house churches were blossoming in residential areas as the police couldn't stop us from meeting in private homes.

In the meantime, we had filed a lawsuit with the High Court, demanding the return of our buildings, and also offering to share services with Kunonga as a way to reconcile the conflict. Ultimately, Justice Rita Makarau ruled in our favor.

We in the CPCA continued to pray for those who had been misled, hoping that they would understand that the church would forever be open to those who chose to come back and knock at its door. Kunonga himself was told that his excommunication did not rule out restoration into the communion if he showed genuine remorse. As an excommunicated bishop, he would not be restored to his former position of holy orders, however, he could have a full lay membership.

Meanwhile, I continued to lead the Diocese of Harare as its caretaker Bishop. Some of our members were arrested and thrown into police cells for days; others were beaten up. Police harassed members when they could at church services.

After Justice Makarau's ruling that the Diocese of Harare had the right to its church buildings, I arrived at the Cathedral to take part in the service under the assumption that Kunonga and his supporters would abide by the court's ruling and would leave. Rut and I arrived toward the end of the 7:30 a.m. service, which Kunonga had held. Riot police were already there, as usual, but we thought our service would go forward without disturbances.

But Kunonga did not leave the Cathedral with his people. Instead, he chose to remain seated at the front of the high altar. Meanwhile, a huge congregation, which had gathered outside, slowly filled up the Cathedral. The servers and I stood in front by the communion rail ready to celebrate the Eucharist.

Just as the Dean of the Cathedral handed over the liturgy book to me so I could start the service, Kunonga stood up in front of the altar and stripped off the altar cloth and candlesticks, showing his utter disregard for the sacredness of the place. He stood there, rolling his eyes under an oversized miter, and said, "Sebastian, this is my cathedral, the cathedral cannot have two bishops." I said, "Yes, you were once the Bishop of the Diocese of Harare, but no longer!" He came toward me, his crozier raised, ready to strike. I looked him straight in the eyes, perhaps a dangerous thing to do as he looked like an insane man. I thought there was some likelihood that I would be badly injured, or even killed. Still, if that was what it took to serve the people of the Diocese of Harare, I was ready. The congregation was stunned, watching all this taking place at the Cathedral altar.

I told Kunonga that we had Makarau's High Court Ruling in our hands to show the law enforcement agents but he said, with utter impunity and defiance, "Who is Makarau?" I thought, surely, the police would arrest him for contempt of the court's judgment. But instead, they advised me to have my congregation continue the Sunday service in the Cathedral Hall. I obliged and led the congregation out of the sanctuary, leaving Kunonga standing in front of the altar, facing the empty cathedral like a museum statue.

The Cathedral seats about 500, and there were at least that many, perhaps more in the church that day to listen to Matthew's Gospel about loving one's enemies. "You have heard that it was said, love your neighbor and hate your enemies. But I tell you, love your enemies and pray for those who persecute you, that you may be children of your Father in heaven" (Matthew

5:43-44). My homily was very brief; the Bible text had all that was required to be said in that situation.

The harassment wasn't over with the confrontation in the Cathedral. The following Sunday at St. Francis Church in Waterfalls, as I was celebrating the Eucharist, the police arrived with their guns, batons, and tear gas. Members of the congregation ran out of the church fearful for their lives. One very pregnant young woman fell several times as she was fleeing and later lost her baby.

The police followed me to St. James Church in Mabvuku the next Sunday, where I was scheduled to celebrate the Eucharist. We started our service peacefully, but when people were coming up to receive Holy Communion, two armed police officers barged into the church. They pointed their guns at the congregants, who began to run out of the church, and then came straight up to the altar with their guns drawn.

I stood there in front of the altar with my ciborium in my hands not knowing what to do and what was to happen next. But I was not a bit scared and just faced them quietly. For some reason, that seemed to disarm them, for they left peacefully. Meanwhile, the congregants were standing some distance from the church, watching what was happening. As soon as the police left, they returned and we continued with our service. When the Eucharist liturgy was over, I delivered a sermon about the cost of discipleship. I said that the cross can be heavy to carry but where and when we carry it, Jesus is there to share our burden with us. He suffers with us as our cross is his cross. We are never alone.

There was more harassment and arrests, especially on Sundays. Even as I arrived home from the confrontation at St. James, word came that our diocesan registrar Michael Chingore had slammed his fist on a police officer's desk and had been thrown into jail at the police station in Mabelreign. I went to get him out and found him locked behind bars. Chingore was a hot-tempered lawyer, but I managed to calm him down and persuaded the police to release him. In Glenview, four members of the Mothers Union had been arrested after a wrangle with the police. In that case, my assistant registrar, Vimbai Nyemba, who was also a lawyer, was successful in arranging for their release. The service given by those lawyers shows that a call to serve people requires a collective response.

I should pause for a moment and acknowledge more of the very committed and competent Christian lawyers that CPCA was fortunate to have as advisers under the leadership of the late Robert Stumbles. Besides the aforementioned Chingore and Nyemba, there was also Eric Matinenga and the law firm of Gill, Godlon and Gerrans.

Not only did we have to contend with the police who were acting at the behest of Kunonga and Mugabe, but we also had problems with judges. Our law firm brought a case before Chief Justice Chambers, who seemed to be listening to our arguments, but, in the end, deferred our case for no good reason. I was so angry that I told him, point-blank, that he should recuse himself from hearing the CPCA case against Kunonga. He angrily told me that as the Chief Justice he was the one who made decisions. I simply said, "Thank you," and left. Another member of the judiciary, who had been a colleague of mine at the University of Zimbabwe, tried to advise us to leave Kunonga to run the diocese by himself, despite knowing that Kunonga had been excommunicated. It made us even more aware that when you have a dictatorial system, even lawyers will abandon their professionalism.

What Kunonga did not understand was that political institutions like Zanu(PF) come and go, but the Church of God remains. He had sold his soul to Zanu(PF), but the party dumped him after six months when they saw that they couldn't use him anymore.

During this whole period when I served as Harare's caretaker Bishop, I felt abandoned by the other Bishops in Zimbabwe and the Church of the Province of Central Africa. They said nothing while CPCA members were persecuted in the Diocese of Harare. It became clearer than ever that being called to be a chief shepherd is a serious call that demands courage, commitment, and dedication as well as being prepared to risk one's life to save the flock. I admire those bishops in church history like Irenaeus, Polycarp, and Justin who, in times of persecution, risked their lives to serve the church from false teachers.

It also reminds me of the story of Jonah and the whale. God called Jonah to go to the great city of Nineveh because the people were living against God's commandments. But Jonah tried to run away, was swallowed up by the whale, and eventually redeemed. Today we don't run away physically, but instead, turn a blind eye to the persecution of our brothers and sisters. Or we see, but we remain silent. That is our Nineveh. I longed for solidarity from my brother bishops in the province but nobody dared to speak out.

However, three bishops from the Anglican Communion came to Zimbabwe to support CPCA members. They included the late Bishop of the Diocese of Massachusetts, Tom Shaw; Archbishop Thabo of the Church Province of South Africa; and Bishop Castle, of the U.K.'s Rochester

Diocese. These people from abroad came to show their solidarity with their sisters and brothers in the Diocese of Harare. They demonstrated their faith in action while my brother bishops in the CPCA did not. The CPCA bishops wouldn't even come to our annual festival celebrating the martyrdom of Bernard Mizeki, an early African missionary, who was killed in 1896, because of his work preaching the Gospel. It was a festival where thousands of the faithful came to celebrate the life of a Christian martyr, yet not one of our Central Province bishops could bring themselves to attend. My brother's bishops missed an opportunity to speak out indignantly against the persecution of the Church. Unless church leadership takes their prophetic role seriously, they face the danger of becoming irrelevant.

Unfortunately, there were also no voices of support from the Zimbabwe Council of Churches and the Catholic Bishops Conference. They had also gone silent because they did not want to be associated with the persecuted CPCA, even though we were fellow members of the Body of Christ. One of the bishops told me he was aware that my members were looking for church halls to hold Sunday services. But he refused on behalf of the Catholic dioceses because he didn't want to be identified with the CPCA. At least he was being truthful, but I also felt sorry for him, so I said to him, politely, "Brother when you have time look at Paul's first letter to the Corinthians, Chapter 2, verse 6, I think you will find it helpful." (In that passage, Paul says: "We do, however, speak a message of wisdom among the mature, but not the wisdom of this age or of the rulers of this age, who are coming to nothing.")

* * *

Rut and the Mothers Union were in the thick of the controversies over Kunonga's attempt to tear apart the church. The leadership of the Union organized women to meet in houses and other places where Kunonga had no access. Rut was busy identifying leaders to undertake leadership training sessions. She organized an all-day meeting for Mothers Union members to meet at St. Michael's church in Mbare and about 800 women came. Rut chose St. Michael's Church as a safe place, thinking that the venue would be safe from police intrusion.

Like me, Rut understood that the call to serve God's people involved risks. She had a very strong belief that faith that wasn't translated into works was dead. At the St. Michael's meeting, which I attended, she tasked team leaders to carry on with Mothers Union activities throughout the diocese.

Just as she was finishing her presentation, four trucks loaded with riot police drove up and started tear-gassing those assembled. This barbaric act brought the gathering to an abrupt end.

A few old ladies who couldn't get up quickly to run away from the police remained seated in their chairs. I went over them to find out if they were injured. One old lady showed me a long scar on her leg that she got when Ian Smith's dogs were set on her during the liberation struggle. She said to me, "Bishop, these riot police are my children. Let them come and kill me, I am not moving from my chair."

What we didn't realize was that a crew from German television was present, secretly filming the proceedings, and by that evening, the police invasion was being televised in Germany. German friends started calling us to find out whether we were safe. Though we were surprised about this development, we were also glad that the persecution of Christians in their church was being made known internationally.

The riot police's actions energized the Mothers Union members—they attacked the wrong people. News of the attack spread. In response, Mothers Union members organized the biggest conference that had ever been held to take place at Belvedere College. The huge attendance at our meetings and house churches made some politicians, who had previously supported Kunonga, realize that Kunonga was losing. On our way from that big Mothers Union conference, Rut and I met a provincial governor, who said, "Bishop, carry on, you are winning." This was the same man I had once hidden in my office at the University of Zimbabwe when riot police were chasing the students all over the campus.

Faith and hope gave Rut the determination and courage to do what needed to be done in what appeared to be a hopeless situation. We were often followed by agents of the Central Intelligence Organization because of our work with the church, though, in a way, we felt rather secure under their spying eyes. We never talked about it at home, but silently, we prayed for our children, relatives, our friends abroad, and the Diocese of Harare.

* * *

In 2009, Chad Gandiya was elected Bishop of the Anglican Diocese of Harare. As caretaker Bishop, I took on the responsibility of organizing his ordination and induction. Kunonga was unaware of these preparations and was busy whipping up the police to invade CPCA churches during Sunday service, as was his usual activity. That had become Kunonga's main Sunday morning duty.

So that we could hold Chad's ordination without interference from the police, I ordered a good lunch for the officers to thank them for keeping the peace during what was expected to be a three-to-four-hour service.

The service was so big that we held it at the Harare Sports Centre, and all went well. It turned out that Kunonga was far away, at a farm, so by the time he heard that it was taking place and sent his police officers, the service was over and Chad was Bishop. We had a small party, organized by my wife, of about ten people who came to bid us farewell. Rut and I left the Diocese of Harare quietly, feeling good to have been instrumental in serving the people during such a difficult time.

CHAPTER TWENTY

Other Ministries, Travels, and Honors

Though I was, once again, officially retired, I still attended to work serving God's people in an organization that I had founded when I was Bishop of Manicaland. Being the Bishop in Manicaland I witnessed extreme poverty in both rural and urban areas. Many of those who lived in such terrible poverty were widows and their children. So, I founded the United Mutare Residents and Ratepayer Trust as a way to address the situation.

Soon after I founded the Trust, a young widow knocked on my door. I recognized her as a member of the Trust and welcomed her in. She cried as she told me her story. Her husband had died of HIV and left her with three children under the age of ten. She said, "Bishop, I don't know what to do. My children are starving, we have no food at home and I do not have anything to give to them, I just don't know what to do. My ten-year-old daughter is no longer going to school. I cannot send her to school hungry otherwise she will faint."

In my profession as a pastor, I had learned to distinguish between genuine and professional beggars. One of the things I noticed was that those who made a profession out of begging never cried. But this widow was heart-stricken. Rut had given me $20 to buy some bread and milk but I gave it to the widow.

Three days later, she returned to tell me that she had bought sugar, mealie meal, tomatoes, dried fish, washing soap, and cooking oil. She had spent quite a bit on the tomatoes, but she explained that she would use them to barter with her neighbors for salt and vegetables from her neighbors. I was sadder than before because it pointed up how destitute her situation was. Her children couldn't go to school because she couldn't afford the school fees.

There are so many widows and single mothers who are in a similar situation in Zimbabwe. We have no national funds to care for the poor. We are nearly forty years in existence as an independent nation, and the government still has not made provisions for its senior citizens, for its widows, and children, let alone provisions for natural disasters like earthquakes, floods, or an epidemic. The idea of being a free country yet still relying on foreign aid is embarrassing, to say the least. Forty years after attaining self-rule, we are still like a banana republic. When a national disaster happens, we are often reduced to beggars. When Cyclone Idai caused so much destruction in 2019, we were utterly dependent on foreign aid, with government emissaries dispatched to ask for help from other countries and from international humanitarian NGOs. And when the disaster aid came, the elite looted it and the real victims were left empty-handed. It was sheer abuse of party politics; an abuse of power, driven by corruption and selfishness.

The UMRRT is there to encourage residents to be generous with each other, even though sharing is so difficult for families who are often reduced to the level of scavengers. We also encourage residents to report to us where there is corruption among city officials causing the poor delivery of services. The big challenge we face as UMRRT is the absence of transparency, accountability, and responsibility within the city council and management—corruption is the worst enemy. We try to instill in residents a sense of ownership of the city and its well-being. Unless we take common responsibility to look after our city, corruption will not stop.

My call to serve the people of God in UMRRT gives me a sense of fulfillment in my vocation to the priesthood. Being engaged in fighting against corruption and exploitation of the poor gives me an urge to carry on doing what I can still manage to do. I cannot fully retire as long as my health allows me to offer some form of service in the community. I cannot remain unconcerned when I see rampant injustice perpetrated by those in power against the powerless. A call to serve God has no room for a passive onlooker or retirement—it is, indeed, a call to total engagement.

* * *

When I was about eight-years-old, I read a book written by a doctor of philosophy, Doctor Aggrey of Achimota College, which was in what was known then as the Gold Coast, which is today's Ghana. I became interested in where the Gold Coast was; I found it in an old atlas on the western part of Africa. Ghana became a faraway place that I always dreamed of visiting, especially Achimota College. But the expense of such a trip kept it only a dream for a long time.

We had become good friends with the Ghanian theologian and professor John Pobee, and his wife, Martha, who was an official in Ghana's foreign service. John came to Zimbabwe frequently as an external examiner for the University of Zimbabwe and our home became his second home in Zimbabwe. When I was elected Bishop of the Diocese Manicaland, I could not think of a better person other than John to preach at my consecration.

In 2007, John and Martha invited me and Rut to celebrate his seventieth birthday in Accra, Ghana, and asked me to preach and preside at the Eucharist birthday celebration. So, my childhood dream of visiting Ghana became a reality. Before his birthday celebration, John took us sightseeing, including Achimota College, which turned out to be a beautiful institution.

We also toured the port of Cape Coast, where John took us to a transit prison where captured slaves were held before they were ready to be shipped to the Americas. The rooms were unbelievably small; only healthy slaves survived the terrible conditions. In the building there was a very narrow corridor, leading to the boat where slaves walked in handcuffs and leg chains, through a door with the inscription "THE DOOR OF NO RETURN." It was human cruelty and historical tragedy at its worst. What upset us most was to know that Christians were very much in the business of the slave trade. The old and ugly building with the door bearing the horrible inscription remains a historical monument for the children who grow up in this village, to help them remember a past episode of Africa's tragic history.

When Rut was taken ill, John and Martha were living in New York where Martha was Ghana's Permanent Representative to the United Nations. Soon after I let them know that Rut's cancer had developed so quickly to an incurable level, she died on October 21, 2017. John wrote the memorial liturgy and would have preached at the service, but having been unwell himself for a long time, his doctors in New York advised him not to take long flights. John died in 2020. Rut and, later, John dying was heartbreaking for our families. However, we continue to cherish fond memories of the ways we celebrated life together.

* * *

In 2008, while we were still in the midst of the struggles in the Diocese of Harare, Rut and I attended the Lambeth Conference. As we left to attend the conference in Canterbury, our hearts were heavy, knowing how the church was being persecuted. We also feared that Kunonga could gain influence during our absence, though, happily, we were wrong in that regard. The spirit of unity among CPCA members had become very strong.

Every ten years, the bishops of the Anglican Communion—about 800 in total—meet in Canterbury, invited by the incumbent British Archbishop. In 2008, the British Archbishop was His Grace, Rowan Williams. Invitations were also extended to ecumenical friends such as the Orthodox Church, the Roman Catholic Church, and the World Council of Churches.

The theme of the conference that year was, "God's Church for God's World; Walking, Listening and Witnessing Together." We had the theme for a year before the conference for study and reflection. Faced with all the current world issues, the Lambeth Conference offered the bishops an opportunity to come and walk, listen, and witness together for God's Church in the World to be involved in the final proclamation of the Gospel.

During the conference, I was amazed by the number of bishops who commiserated with me about my diocese being persecuted by Mugabe. One bishop in my group of about fifty bishops stood up and shouted so that everybody in the room wouldn't miss what he was saying: "Mugabe the dictator, should leave the church of God alone." In my group, John Sentamu, the Archbishop of York, and I were tasked to draft a resolution about the persecuted Church in Harare Diocese.

During the conference, Archbishop Rowan also asked me to organize my fellow bishops from Zimbabwe to give testimonies before the Eucharist service. But when I sat down with those bishops, they declined to do so, because they feared that they would be arrested when they returned home. I was left alone to speak about my diocese. It was a lonely feeling indeed that my fellow bishops from Zimbabwe would not speak with me. I suggested that they read Paul's letter to the church at Corinth where he says, "If one part suffers, every part suffers with it" (1 Corinthians 12:25).

Though I was disappointed at the behavior of my fellow Zimbabwean bishops and by the way some bishops behaved like tourists, instead of doing the work of the conference, I also felt renewed by those who were truly making good on the gift of walking, listening, and witnessing together.

And I was not arrested on my arrival at the airport in Harare to the great embarrassment of my brother's bishops.

Something else happened that was momentous in 2008: I was awarded the Swedish Par Anger prize—a tremendous honor that was entirely unexpected.

The Per Anger Prize is given by the Swedish government in honor of Ambassador Per Anger for the risks he took in helping Jews secretly leave the country during World War II. The Per Anger Prize was established in 2004, in his memory to promote initiatives supporting the fight for human rights and democracy.

Never would I have thought that my work in Zimbabwe would come to the notice of the Per Anger prize committee. Yes, I opened my mouth, sometimes very loudly, to condemn the perpetrators of injustice because I felt so strongly that I could not turn a blind eye to injustice. I thought that it was my call to do so.

I will never forget the day that I found out about the award. The Swedish Ambassador, Sten Rylander, and his wife Berit had often invited me and Rut to the embassy for their country's national celebrations. So, on this occasion, when they invited us, we thought it was for another national holiday celebration. But when we arrived at their residence, we discovered there were no other cars besides the ambassador's. We apologized, thinking that we had come too early, only to be asked to come in and take a seat in the lounge. Mrs. Rylander served us drinks, and we continued to wonder when other guests would be arriving. But nobody came. Finally, Sten arrived and we went in for lunch. I was asked to say grace, which I did. When I finished saying grace, but before the meal was served, Stan broke the news about my having been awarded the Per Anger Prize. Both Rut and I were speechless.

We were tremendously touched to be so honored by the Swedish government. The Ambassador then informed us that the prize would be awarded to me in Stockholm. Rut and I were delighted to be going back to Stockholm, to the city where we met so many years ago during the World Council of Churches conference in 1968.

We flew to Stockholm via Frankfurt where we picked up our youngest daughter, Rufaro, and then we arrived in Stockholm where we met our second daughter, Tinao, who joined us from London. We were greeted by Ambassador Rylander, who accompanied us to the offices of the minister of the local government, who was a very charming lady. In the evening there was, of course, a reception hosted by the minister of Foreign Affairs, also a woman. Both ministers were wonderful ladies—unassuming, and caring. It was evident that they were committed to their work.

It was an evening of speeches. In my speech, I talked about my parishioner, Jestina Mukoko, who was missing after having been kidnapped from her home in the middle of the night. I talked about Itai Dzamara, a young activist and critic of Mugabe, who I had come to know and like, who had also disappeared.

I concluded by saying that this was not the kind of government the Swedish people had supported during the liberation struggle. This was not the Zimbabwe we fought for to remove Ian Smith. We fought to live in a country that has space for everybody, a country that respects human rights, a country where citizens don't fear being tortured or kidnapped. I felt these current stories would help the Swedish people understand what was going on in Zimbabwe and the atrocities being committed by the regime.

During our stay in Stockholm, we enjoyed VIP treatment and were treated most graciously. But it was the chance to retrace our footsteps in the city where we met thirty years before that was the dearest to us.

Ambassador Rylander tried to publicize the award in Zimbabwe, but he was denied media access. It was not in the regime's interest to let the citizens of Zimbabwe know that one of their chief critics had been given such a prestigious award.

* * *

There were other travels, to Australia, where I went at the invitation of the Hon. Dr. Reverend F. Nile, a charismatic Pentecostal leader who wanted me to bear personal testimony about the persecution of Anglicans in Zimbabwe. Though Rev. Nile tried to arrange an invitation for me to meet the Anglican Archbishop of Sydney while I was there, an invitation was not forthcoming. I wasn't surprised as the Archbishop and I didn't see eye-to-eye about gay people; he was very conservative. But the Assistant Anglican Bishop who came to see me preach invited me to visit him. Michael Darby, who was my guide and responsible for my schedule, came with me. To my surprise, the assistant bishop was different from the Archbishop and was sympathetic to the struggles Zimbabwe was going through. Darby said to the Assistant Bishop, "Bishop Bakare is restoring the Diocese of Harare to the CPCA. He was invited to come and share his story with us in this country. Christians in this country, who want to help the Bishop, can do so. Help if you so wish, but he will not ask for help." I thanked the Bishop for his time and for listening to my story. And then, to my surprise, the next day, the Bishop called me asking what kind of help he could offer. I told him that I needed transport to take me around the diocese, and he generously sent us about AU$15,000, which we used to buy a second-hand truck. At the same time, my alma mater, the Church Divinity School of the Pacific sent a donation, which we used to buy a car for the Bishop's office; it's still used by the Bishop. I appreciated the invitation from Rev. Nile and Darby and I remain grateful for their hospitality. The Diocese of Harare received this donation with gratitude from their concerned sisters and brothers in Australia and the United States.

* * *

Rut and I were fortunate to receive honorary doctorates from two institutions for our service to the church in Zimbabwe and the wider world. One was from my seminary, the Church Divinity School of the Pacific in Berkeley in May of 2009, and the other from the General Theological Seminary in New York.

It was amazing to return to Berkeley twenty-seven years after we earned our Master's degrees, to receive honorary doctorates. It was an occasion to remember as our names were called to go forward to receive our crowns, in a sense. And it was a moment of great joy and excitement to have my professors, fellow students, and alumni hear me preach on one of my favorite themes: "Hope against hope," meaning that the resurrection of Jesus Christ gives us hope against hope. In my conclusion, I said that it was hope that kept my people alive in Zimbabwe as we continued to live, year after year, under a repressive system.

Rut, I, and our children had always cherished our memories of the seminary community in Berkeley, so it meant so much to us to receive these honorary doctorates. And there was more joy to come. The following week we flew to New York where I baptized our granddaughter, Nomsa Elizabeth, the child of our eldest daughter Nyasha and her husband Alain, at St. Mark's Episcopal Church in Brooklyn.

The second honorary doctorates for Rut and me were given by the General Theological Seminary in New York City. It was another glamorous occasion. When the citation was read before the degrees were awarded, I was amazed at the author's knowledge of the situation in Zimbabwe and our roles in the struggle. But it was written by the Rev. Andrew Kadel, who was the seminary's Library Director, and my classmate, many years ago at

CDSP. He had kept track of all that had transpired in Zimbabwe since we had known each other back then.

CHAPTER TWENTY-ONE

Born-Frees

M y dear "Born-Frees"—and by that expression I mean my Zimbabwe
brothers and sisters who were born knowing only Independence—
what you see and experience today is a result of a series of destructive epi-
sodes in the history of our country. Our history is a shattered one, though
there is also tremendous resilience. The first destruction was by British Settlers who invaded our land and took it away from our forebears. The second
is a shattered dream by the so-called liberation heroes who, like their white
settler predecessors, have taken the land and kept it for themselves. A free
and liberated Zimbabwe is still an illusion for the majority of our people. I
can rightly say that the one thing my generation achieved was the right to
vote. Today, the right to vote is the only positive legacy we leave to you and
those yet unborn.

Living under colonial regimes had its challenges including being
viewed by the white settlers as not being fully human and having no rights.
Whites had no respect for black people. Blacks were treated as commodi-
ties that were to be used, abused, discarded, and condemned. Blacks had
no recourse to legal protections. Land which provided them a source of
livelihood was forcefully taken away from them. No land, no rights; we
were completely disempowered. That deprivation of land and the means
to have meaningful lives forced my generation into the liberation struggle
to reclaim the land from the invaders, a subject I wrote about at length in
my book "My Right to Land." Despite repression and violence from the
white regime, my generation achieved its goal of political independence.
Unfortunately, economic freedom didn't follow. Your task as Born-Frees is

to work hard to achieve total emancipation for all and not only for the elite. The current post-independence leadership thrives on denying the majority access to national resources. Leadership that is greedy, selfish, and corrupt can never create a system that offers equal opportunity to all.

The other fact about the liberation struggle is that even as Africans sought to oust the white invaders, there were also serious tribal conflicts over who would lead the country after independence. These tribal conflicts could turn violent—Herbert Chitepo and Josiah Tongogara died because of the raging tribalism. The Reverend Ndabaningi Sithole was sidelined under flimsy pretexts, but the real reason was ongoing tribal conflict. *Gukurahundi* was a massacre of the Ndebele People based on tribalism. You will have to work hard to face the old enemies of totemism, clannism, tribalism, and provincialism. These all still play a significant role today in our society. It is likely to take a long time before they disappear, but they need to be overcome if true freedom, especially economic freedom can be achieved.

During the colonial era preference for employment opportunities was based on color, a black applicant was the least considered. Today, job seekers are often confronted by the interviewer with the question, "Where do you come from?" Unless you come from the province of the interviewer, chances are you won't get the job. It's a vicious circle that gives employment to the favored ones, instead of the most qualified ones.

Sociologists tell us that culture is dynamic, and if that is so, your task is to be involved in that process of cultural dynamism. And you will need to work toward a culture of selfless leadership, a leadership that is people centered. When Mugabe took leadership of the new Republic of Zimbabwe, we thought that he was a gift to the nation. I remember a Zanu(PF) mayor of Harare saying, that as a son of God, it was his job to serve God and the people. But during his time in office this self-professed son of God turned out to be the opposite. He sold his soul to wealth accumulation. He remained a captive to his clan and deprived the nation of nurturing democratic principles. In that he was like Mugabe who grabbed everything within reach for himself.

Your challenge as Born-Frees is to transform and create the second Republic of Zimbabwe for all, a Zimbabwe that develops a vibrant economy. Where everybody has equal opportunity to contribute and benefit from national resources, where everybody has the freedom to choose and pursue his or her goals without being prejudiced by various tribal or clan, or provincial affiliations.

As for you, cherish the little and limited freedom you have compared to what my generation went through. Your agenda is to create an environment that safeguards human rights and security, a rule of law where nobody is above the law, where political leadership does not act with impunity, where, above everything else, peace and justice are the core values of the nation. It is also important to note that no repressive regime can survive forever. Dictators come and go, leaving an indelible, negative mark behind them but the nation remains. All that dictators can leave behind is a negative legacy and a name people will want to forget as soon as they disappear from the position of power. This is a fact.

I invite you, Born-Frees, to serve Zimbabwe from where it is today. Zimbabwe needs you to redeem the nation from its decadent leadership committed to serving. Selfishness, corruption, and greed displayed by our liberation leaders and their cronies will not simply vanish overnight unless you have a vision of what you want this nation to look like in the future. My generation after attaining independence has abused national resources. Yours is a mammoth task before you.

May I remind you that although the politics of this country are repressively ugly, bear in mind that dictators come and go but the nation remains. My generation passes the baton to you that you may continue to run the race. Although the situation is unbearable today, the future may still be different. It remains in your hands.

* * *

Fifty-nine years have elapsed since I was ordained to the diaconate in 1961. I am unable to see my footprints where I am coming from and the direction I still have to take. I stand at a crossroads between life and death but for now, the window remains open and I can still see the endless horizon. I am convinced that God will take me to my destination when that moment comes. Meanwhile, I look forward each day to new experiences as they come within my reach. So far, my journey has provided me with joyful moments and sad—the saddest being the untimely passing on of my dear companion, Rut. I miss her every day. My faith in God has taken me to the top of the mountain as well as into the valley. I have been blessed to come into contact with people who have made my life so rich and have given me, and still give me spiritual provision for my pilgrimage. Here and there I encountered the devil among religious and political leaders, but I don't regret those encounters either. I still hold on to the belief that God is not finished with me and I will carry on doing what he wants me to do.

Again, in the words of the Zimbabwe National Anthem by the writer and poet S.M. Mutsvairo, this expresses so well the natural beauty of our land:

> *O lift the banner,*
> *The flag of Zimbabwe is the symbol of freedom proclaiming victory;*
> *We praise our heroes' sacrifice, and vow to keep our land free from foes;*
> *And may the Almighty protect and bless our land.*
> *O lovely Zimbabwe so wondrously adorned with mountains,*
> *Rivers cascading, flowing free.*
> *May rain abound, and fertile fields;*
> *May we be fed, our labor blessed;*
> *May the Almighty protect and bless our land;*
> *The land of our fathers bestowed upon us all;*
> *From Zambezi to Limpopo;*
> *May our leaders be exemplary;*
> *May the Almighty protect and bless our land.*

Many years ago, when I asked Mutsvairo the meaning of his poem, he said, "It is my prayer for Zimbabwe. I pray that Zimbabwe cherishes the hard-won freedom we longed for many years. Yes, indeed, it is my prayer."

The following Sunday, in the university chapel, I used the very words of the national anthem as a prayer for the nation. When a student pointed out that I was praying the words of our national anthem, I said, "Yes; our national anthem is a prayer for us all."

Born-Free, your challenge is to engage in a struggle that seeks to achieve genuine freedom in Zimbabwe for all. Like Isaiah, the God of yesterday, today, and tomorrow still say to us, "Who shall go for us to liberate Zimbabwe from the sin of corruption and selfishness?" Unless you respond to the call to serve our people, the desire to live in a free and democratic Zimbabwe will remain an elusive dream. What I have written in this memoir are a few things that affected me from my childhood to this day. I wrote this for your benefit, my children, including the unborn and all the Born-Frees. Wherever you are, whoever you are, female or male, it does not matter which province you come from, which tribe, clan, or totem you hold: Zimbabwe is your country and your birthright. God calls you from wherever you are to serve your people.

This is my prayer for your generation:

Lord God our Mother, Father, and Redeemer
Endow upon children of this beautiful land of Zimbabwe
The gift of faith and confidence to hear you when you call them to
serve your people.
Give them the tenacity and courage to hold on to you, despite the
hardships they may endure
Give them sufficient grace never to give up what you desire them
to have
Remove stony hearts from those who are called to lead our nation
Give them the spirit of humility and selflessness
Provide them with political leadership that has people at the heart
May you be on the side of your people who so much feel abandoned
As always in times of suffering
In times of oppression and denial of human rights
May you be on their side as you were yesterday in the liberation
struggle,
Today and tomorrow as they still long for peace and justice.
You are our God. May we forever abide in you
OH! God bless Zimbabwe
Bless Africa
Bless our world and heal it from its brokenness
Amen.

Afterword

R ut had been writing her memoir for some time which she left unfinished. When we read her memoir after she died, we discovered that she quoted the Biblical Naomi and her daughter-in-law, Ruth, as having a profound impact on her. Ruth, in the Hebrew language truth, means companion, friend, or as I chose to call the woman I met forty-eight years ago, Rut, which is the name I use in this memoir.

Rut developed a passion for Zimbabwe from the time of the liberation struggle in 1972. When we finally came to the country, she adopted Zimbabwe and became a citizen. She lived the words of the Biblical Ruth: Where you go, I will go, and where you dwell, there will I dwell. Your people will be my people, and your God my God. I hope I have been able to capture a little of Rut's caring for and dedication to the people of Zimbabwe.

Rut was in terrible pain from the cancer that claimed her life. One day she asked me: "Sebastian, what did I do to deserve to suffer like this; I cannot bear this anymore." Those are words I will remember as long as I live.

We talked for a moment about Jesus being crucified and how he cried from the pain and the sense of being abandoned. And how, though he was in agony, he still had faith and hope in his Father and prayed: "Father, into your hands I commend myself." I quoted from Psalm 22, about God responding to our cries for help, but Rut didn't answer. Sometimes I think perhaps I shouldn't have talked to her about God's love at that moment; she was hurting so terribly. I failed to put myself in her shoes, but I thought that it would help to remind her of her great faith in God. When she said to me, "Sebastian, what did I do to deserve to suffer like this; I cannot bear this anymore," it didn't mean she had no faith in God. She was seeking affirmation of God's love, the God she believed in so deeply, the God who had come closer to her in the last moments of her life.

The following day, in the early hours, Rut passed on. There were two nurse's aides attending to her; sadly, I wasn't at her side when she died. When I came in at dawn to check on her, she was already gone. How I wished she had waited for me just to say a few last words before her final departure. Though I and her daughters were in the same house, she was now far away from us, far away from her native country, dying and now ready to be buried in the country of her husband, a country she had adopted as her own. Like Ruth in the Bible, her wish was fulfilled: "Where you die, I will die and there I will be buried."

Below is a prayer she wrote when we were together with the faithful members of the Church of the Province of Central Africa at a time when we were being persecuted by Mugabe's police under the command of the rebellious and excommunicated Bishop Kunonga. Bishop Chad Gandiya kindly adopted it for Rut's memorial service.

Whoever we are and whether black or white, rich or poor, free or not free, we shall become what God wants us to be.

Rut's prayer:

> Lord, we are here to remember your suffering until death.
> Lord our people are suffering, hungry, persecuted, and threatened.
> Lord, you have commissioned us to be the light of the world.
> Let us be what you want us to become. Amen.